D1371583

FROM DEATH TO LIFE

CHRISTOPH SCHÖNBORN, O.P.

FROM DEATH TO LIFE

The Christian Journey

Translated by
Brian McNeil, C.R.V.

IGNATIUS PRESS   SAN FRANCISCO

Title of the German original:
Existenz im Übergang:
Pilgerschaft, Reinkarnation, Vergöttlichung
Einsiedeln, Trier: Johannes Verlag, 1988

Cover art: Sinai, Icon with Crucifixion
Photo © 1978, Alexandria–Michigan–Princeton Expedition
to Mount Sinai
Reprinted by permission of George Braziller, Inc.
from *The Icon* by Kurt Weitzman

Cover design by Riz Boncan Marsella

To
Dorothee Welp
in gratitude

CONTENTS

FOREWORD

"But our homeland is in heaven, whence we also await the Savior, our Lord Jesus Christ" (Phil 3:20). Is the yearning for a life beyond death the fundamental mood of the earliest Church—the expectation of the end of the world on the part of a little flock of the chosen ones, in flight from the world, which is too narrow and too hostile to them, so that they cannot find any undisturbed joy in it?

The charge that Christianity is a contempt for the earth that transposes consolation into a life beyond death runs like a red thread through the history of anti-Christian polemics, from Celsus to Nietzsche. And it is a fact that Christian proclamation has been filled from early days with the yearning for heavenly fulfillment: "Seek the things that are above, where Christ is, seated at the right hand of God. Strive to attain what is above, not what is on earth" (Col 3:1–2). Let us quote *Augustine* as a representative of the countless preachers who have lived and proclaimed this "existence in transition": "Thus, we are still on the way. Wherever we may come, we must still pass on further [*transire*], until we reach the goal. 'We know that we shall be like him, when he appears; for we shall see him as he is' (1 Jn 3:2). That is the goal. There, there is eternal praise, there an eternal, unceasing alleluia." [1] There are two lives, one *here*, the other *there*. We live correctly *here* only to the extent that we do not lose sight, in all the *now* (*nunc*), of the *then* (*tunc*). Augustine speaks again and again of these "two lives" (*duae vitae*):

una in fide,	*altera in specie;*
una in tempore peregrinationis,	*altera in aeternitate mansionis;*
una in labore,	*altera in requie;*
una in via,	*altera in patria;*
una in opere actionis,	*altera in mercede contemplationis.* [2]

("We live the one life in faith, / the other in vision; // the one in the time of pilgrimage, / the other in the eternity of abiding; // the one in toil, / the other in rest; // the one *en route*, / the other in our native land; // the one in the work of activity, / the other in the reward of contemplation.")

We ought to be cautious about dismissing this attitude toward life all too quickly as contempt for the world. All this does indeed sound like a flight from the world, yet these men did not despise creation, and while they spoke of this world as a "valley of tears", they were at the same time aware of its beauty; they cultivated it, built cathedrals, and created works that continue to nourish us even today.

[1] *In Ep. Ioa. Tract.* x, 6: PL 35, 2058.

[2] *In Ioa. Tract.* CXXIV, 5, 7; CCL 36, 685, 82–87; cf. *En. in Ps.* CXLVIII, 1; CCL 40, 2165, 10–35; cf. also below Chapter 3, nn. 16–22.

How could a man with such zest for living, so famous for his humor, such a lover of music as Saint Philip Neri (the "inventor" of the Oratory) write the following sonnet?

> Qual prigion la ritien ch'indi partire
> non possa, e al fin coi piei calcar le stelle
> e viver sempr' in dio e a se morire? [3]

("What prison holds the soul back so that it cannot depart from hence, so that it finally can trample the stars under its feet and live forever in God and die to itself?")

This is where the Marxist critique of religion makes its attack: religion distracts men from earthly distress; eschatological hope makes them incapable of resistance and submissive.[4] It is here that Nietzsche above all strikes home: "The concept of 'life beyond death', a 'true world', is invented in order to devalue the *only* world that exists—so that our earthly reality is left with no goal, no reason, and no task." [5]

Today, language about man's pilgrim path, about his homeland in heaven, of earthly tribulation and hope for life beyond death, has become largely a foreign language in the Christian churches. It is only seldom that a

---

[3] Quoted in L. Ponnelle and L. Bordet, *Saint Philippe Néri et la société romaine de son temps (1515–1595)* (Paris, 1928), 525.

[4] Gusine Schwan, *L. Kolakowski—eine marxistische Philosophie der Freiheit* (Stuttgart, 1971), 33.

[5] *Werke* (Schlechta) (Munich, n.d.), II, 1159.

sermon dares to look out on the vista of eternal life. It
seems that fear of being accused of dispensing a consolation in a life after death and of fleeing from the world
has become to a large extent a self-censorship (for the
most part, no doubt, something of which the speaker is
not aware).[6] The silence about the heavenly dimension
of our faith, of course, has consequences. Is not this "eschatological amnesia" of our preaching one reason why
many people no longer turn to the Church when they
want information about the "last things"? The growing
interest in spiritualist practices, esoteric doctrines, belief
in reincarnation, and many other such things is alarm-
ing.

The texts collected in this short book attempt to
reflect in various areas on the significance of the eschatological dimension of our Faith. They are attempts to
ask the tradition attentively about the knowledge and
the experiences of matters of living and dying that it
bears—often these are like buried treasures that must
first be brought to the surface afresh today. The link
that unites these various essays is the concern to find in
Jesus Christ himself the focal point of the *Christian* vision of life on earth and life after death. He is the Alpha
and the Omega, origin and goal. It is he who discloses
to us what "existence in transition" means.

[6] Max Thürkauf observes (*Die Tränen des Herrn Galilei* [Zurich, 1978],
109): "Today's natural scientists believe so firmly in the heaven of the
astronomers that the theologians scarcely dare any longer to believe in
their old traditional heaven."

Thus, our *first chapter* has its starting point in Christ. The incarnate, crucified, and risen Son of God *remains man forever*; he, the God–Man, therefore is and remains the living bridge between heaven and earth, time and eternity. The fulfillment of the world has already become reality in him.

The *second chapter* complements the first. The goal of the Incarnation of God is the "deification" of man. What this means we shall discover in the light of the tradition of the Fathers and of mysticism. Christ himself is the form and content of the deification of man.

As Christ unites in himself heaven and earth and gives time its secure place in eternity, so also does the *Church*, which is his Body (*third chapter*). As a *pilgrim Church*, she belongs indeed to the earthly reality, but—inseparably from this—she is also already the *heavenly Church*. Seen from the perspective of Christ, her Head, she is the place of God's dominion: the *kingdom of God*.

As "seed and beginning of the kingdom of God", she comes into time, she grows visibly and tangibly in time, yet she is not "of this world". This inevitably leads to tensions with the "kingdoms" of this world. Thus, the theme of our *fourth chapter* is *the relationship between the Church and politics* in view of the coming of God's kingdom.

In the *fifth chapter*, we take up one of the most acute eschatological questions: *the doctrine of reincarnation*. Why has this view of the relationship between earthly life and life beyond the grave remained alien to the Christian Faith? Why did the early Church reject the doctrine of reincarnation? What "fundamental experience" causes Christian Faith to see death and life after death in another light?

The *sixth chapter* shows that the Christian tradition certainly does know of a "migration of the soul", naturally of a very specific kind. The ancient *rites accompanying death* know about the path taken (once only) by the soul out of this world into the other world. By disclosing to us the meaning of dying, they also show us the path of life, so that we may "live soberly, righteously, and piously in this world, while we await the blessed fulfillment of our hope: namely, the appearing of the glory of our great God and Savior Christ Jesus" (Titus 2:12–13).

> Notre Dame de Vie
> July 22, 1987
> Feast of Saint Mary Magdalen

Chapter I

"GOD WANTS TO REMAIN A MAN FOREVER": ON THE MEANING OF THE ARTICLE OF THE CREED: "HE SITS AT THE RIGHT HAND OF THE FATHER"

John Damascene, who synthesizes the great tradition of the Greek Fathers in *An Exact Exposition of the Orthodox Faith*, sets out the meaning of this article of the Creed as follows:

> We say, "Christ sits bodily at the right hand of God the Father", but we do not teach the existence of any localized right hand of the Father. For how could he who cannot be circumscribed possess a localized right hand? For it is only circumscribed beings that have a right and a left hand. No, when we speak of the right hand of the Father, we understand this to mean the splendor and glory of the Godhead, in which the Son of God exists from eternity as God and consubstantial with the Father, and in which he now, after having become flesh in these last times, also sits bodily, since his flesh has been glorified along with him.

The chapter title quotation is from A. Grillmeier, *Jesus der Christus im Glauben der Kirche*, vol. 1 (Freiburg, 1979), 774.

For he is adored together with his flesh in an act of adoration on the part of the entire creation.[1]

In this brief exposition, the two most important statements of the Faith are summarized, which the early Church saw as confirmed by the credal article about "sitting at the right hand of the Father": that Christ is God, "consubstantial with the Father", and that he has not given up his humanity after his glorification but truly sits "bodily" at the right hand of the Father. A number of more ecclesiological consequences are connected to these two fundamental christological affirmations; John Damascene does not mention them specifically here, but these are richly developed by the Fathers. At issue here above all are the lordship and the judicial role of Christ, the believers' sharing in Christ's lordship, and the unity of Head and Body, of Christ and Church.

A glance at the significance of this credal article in the history of dogma shows, perhaps to the surprise of some readers, that this article, which gives the impression of being rather inoffensive and marginal, in reality synthesizes, as a magnifying glass focuses the sun's rays, the totality of the Christian Faith. First, let us listen to some witnesses of the "rule of faith", who present unpolemically the meaning of this article of the Creed. Then we shall present (in the second section) some examples of christological controversies about the mean-

[1] *Expos. fidei* IV, 2; PG 94, 1104 D.

ing of the *sessio ad dexteram Patris*. Finally, in the third section, I wish to bring out the ecclesiological aspect of this mystery of Christ, above all with Augustine as our point of departure. In these three sections, we can give only brief references, as it were "samples", from the treasury of the Church Fathers.

1. Witnesses of the "Rule of Faith"

As is the case already in the New Testament, the statements about Christ's sitting at the right hand of God are connected in the early Church too with the Easter faith and with the *confession* of faith. In the Easter homily of Bishop *Melito of Sardis* (ca. 160–70), we find a solemn profession of faith in Christ that is entirely filled with the certainty of Christ's paschal victory and, beyond this, of his eternal lordship:

> This is he
> who made heaven and earth
> and formed man at the beginning;
> who was announced through the law and the
>   prophets;
> who became flesh through a virgin;
> who was hanged on the wood;
> who was buried in the earth;
> who rose from the dead
> and ascended to the heights of heaven;
> who sits at the right hand of the Father;

    who has all authority to judge and to save;
    through whom the Father made everything
    from the beginning unto all ages.[2]

Far from all polemics, Christ is confessed here, as the sequence of the text says, as "beginning and end", "unutterable beginning and incomprehensible end", as King and Lord, as Alpha and Omega.[3] *Irenaeus of Lyons*, too, at the end of the second century, emphasizes that the preexistent Son of God is at the same time the crucified and glorified One, against the tendency of the gnostics to divide Christ into an earthly being and a heavenly being: "The one whom Paul identifies with complete clarity as Christ, the Son of God, is none other than the one who was arrested and suffered and shed his blood for us, he who also rose and was taken up into heaven, as he himself says: 'Christ, who died, or even more, who was raised up and is at the right hand of God' (Rom 8:34). . . . One and the same is Jesus Christ, the Son of God, who reconciled us to God through his suffering and who rose from the dead, who is at the right hand of the Father and is perfect in all things."[4] *Fulgentius of Ruspe* (beginning of the sixth century) emphasizes in his "Letter to Peter about the

[2] *Peri Pascha* 104.

[3] Ibid., 105, 130.

[4] *Adv. haer.* III, 16, 9. Like Melito before him, Irenaeus too interprets the New Testament's "at the right hand of God" as "at the right hand of the Father"; cf. O. Perler, in Méliton de Sardes, *Sur la Pâque, Sources Chrétiennes* 123 (Paris, 1966), 208.

correct rule of faith" precisely this identity: "One and the same God, the Son of God . . . according to the flesh that lay in the grave, rose from the grave; and the same incarnate God ascended to heaven on the fortieth day after the Resurrection and sits at the right hand of God." [5] We can read in *Cyril of Jerusalem* what the catechumens in Jerusalem were told in the catecheses on the Faith before their baptism. He speaks in three places of the significance of the "sitting at the right hand of the Father", emphasizing each time that Christ sits from all eternity at the right hand of the Father, "for it is not the case, as some have held, that he was in some sense crowned by God after his suffering; nor did he gain the throne at the right hand because of his patient endurance; rather, he has possessed the royal dignity for as long as he has existed—but he is begotten eternally— and shares the Father's throne, since he is, as we have said, God, wisdom and power. He reigns together with the Father and has created everything for the sake of the Father." [6] The accent here lies wholly on the divinity of Christ, which is given prominence precisely through the "sharing the throne": "*One* Son is to be proclaimed, who sits before time at the right hand of the Father, and has not received this position of sitting at his side only little by little, in time, after his suffering." [7] While Cyril scarcely mentions the "conglorification" of Christ's hu-

---

[5] PL 65, 677 AB.

[6] IV Catechesis, no. 7.

[7] XI Catechesis, no. 17; cf. XIV Catechesis, nos. 27–30.

manity, this stands strongly in the foreground in Pope *Leo the Great*'s sermons on the Ascension. He invites his hearers to rejoice with the disciples that "human nature has taken its place high above all the creatures of heaven . . . in order to find the ultimate goal of its elevation on the throne of the eternal Father and to share on this throne the glory of him [i.e., the Father] with whose being it was linked through the Son." All men are in a certain sense, "implicitly", given a share in the humanity of Christ in this glorification: "Christ's Ascension means our own elevation", for God's Son has "incorporated" human nature into himself and "given it a place at the right hand of the Father".[8]

Thus, the most important questions of the Faith find expression in the exposition of this article of the Faith: Jesus' divinity, his consubstantiality with the Father; his humanity, which is not abolished at the Resurrection but rather brought to perfection; the unity of the divinity and humanity of Christ even now in his eternal lordship; the identity of the one Son, Jesus Christ, through all the "stages" of salvation history.

This is what the *regula fidei*, the guiding line of the Faith, says, but naturally, questions are not lacking. Is it possible to believe seriously, with John Damascene, in a *bodily* "sitting at the right hand"? Is it possible to conceive of Christ's consubstantial existence as God? *Augustine* reminds the catechumens (and us with them!) at this point that faith is the presupposition for under-

[8] *Sermo* 73, 4.

standing: "Christ ascended into heaven. Believe! He sits
at the right hand of the Father. Believe! . . . He is there!
Do not let your heart say, 'What is he doing?' Do not
ask what we are not permitted to find out! He is there!
That is enough for you! He is in bliss, and it is from the
bliss that is called 'the right hand of the Father' that the
name of this bliss is derived: 'the right hand of the Father'." [9] "Thus to be at the right hand means the same
as to be in the highest bliss, where there are righteousness, peace, and joy; just as the goats are assigned their
place at the left hand (Mt 25:33), i.e., in wretchedness,
because of their labors and torments for unrighteous-
ness. Thus, when we speak of God's 'sitting', this does
not denote a bodily position but the judicial authority
that is never lacking to his lordship, but that continuously administers to each one what he deserves." [10]
Thomas Aquinas will take over from Augustine this met-
aphorical interpretation of the "right hand" as bliss and
as judicial authority.[11] But does not this use of meta-
phor threaten the realism of the *abiding* bodiliness of
Christ? Augustine does not wish to dissolve this in allegory. But he also points to the incomprehensibility of
this article of the Faith: "Where and in what manner
the body of the Lord exists in heaven is surely the most

[9] *Sermo ad catechumenos* IV, 11; PL 40, 634.

[10] *De fide et symbolo* VII, 14; PL 40, 188.

[11] *Summa theologiae* III, q. 57; *Comp. theol.* c. 241; and other texts.
Thomas quotes the fine words from Augustine's *Sermo ad catechumenos*:
"But there, in the eternal bliss, everything is 'at the right hand', because
there is no misery there": q. 57, a. 1 ad 2.

inquisitive and superfluous question. It suffices simply to believe that he is in heaven. Our weakness is not permitted to seek to penetrate the mysteries of heaven; rather, it belongs to our faith to think high and reverent thoughts of the dignity of the body of the Lord." [12]

2. The Article of Faith in Controversy

Precisely this—thinking "high and reverent thoughts" of the body of Christ—met resistance early on. It is worthwhile to look briefly at the exposition of this article given by the gnostics of the second century. [13] The fundamental conviction of *gnosis*, repeated again and again, is that "redemption concerns only the soul, for all that the body can do, in keeping with its nature, is to fall into decay." [14] The gnostics liked to appeal to Paul's words, "Flesh and blood cannot inherit the kingdom of God" (1 Cor 15:50), in support of their view that there cannot exist any salvation or eternal perfection for the body as a part of the material world. [15] Thus most of the gnostics understand the Ascension of Christ too as the return of the heavenly Christ into his original, purely spiritual condition. For example, the gnostic Apelles taught that Christ formed a body for himself from the

[12] *De fide et symbolo* v, 131; PL; Perl, 23.

[13] Detailed exposition in A. Orbe, *Cristologia Gnostica*, vol. II (Madrid, 1976), 535–73.

[14] Irenaeus, *Adv. haer.* I, 24, 5 (on Basilides).

[15] Ibid., v, 9ff.

various cosmic materials, that this body was crucified, and that he showed it to the disciples after his Resurrection. But "after this, he left his body behind; he gave it back to the earth from which it came. He did not take anything alien with him but gave back to its own everything that he had made use of for a time, when he unloosed the bonds of the body: he gave what was warm back to what was warm, what was cold to what was cold, what was liquid to what was liquid, what was solid to what was solid: then he went to the good Father, leaving behind the seed of life in the world to the believers through his disciples." [16] It is a gnostic principle that everything must return again to its original place.[17] What is matter must once again dissolve itself in matter; what is spirit returns—without fail—to spirit. Hermogenes (not a gnostic, properly speaking, but representative here for the gnostic interpretation of the Ascension) teaches that Christ "was raised after his suffering, appeared bodily to the disciples, and left his body behind in the sun when he ascended to heaven, while himself coming to the Father". He appeals here to Psalm 18: "He has set up a tent in the sun", interpreting the "tent" here as the "earthly tent" of the body.[18] This cosmology may appear foreign, but the kernel of the affirmation is clear: it is impossible, in broad circles of the cultivated classical world, to con-

[16] Hippolytus, *Ref.* vii, 38; Orbe, *Cristologia Gnostica*, 538.

[17] Cf. Irenaeus, *Adv. haer.* ii, 14, 4.

[18] According to Hippolytus, *Ref.* viii, 17.

ceive of a *bodily* resurrection, of an eternal perfecting of
the *body*. Accordingly, it must be denied that the "sitting at the right hand" has any bodily aspect whatever.
Rather, in gnosis the "right hand" is now considered as
an expression for "spiritual", "higher", "full of light",
and "masculine", while the "left hand" represents the
opposite of all this. Consequently, some gnostics interpret Christ's sitting at the right hand of God to mean
that Christ is *higher* than God, i.e, than *this* God, who
speaks to the Jews in the Old Testament and says in
Psalm 110:1: "Sit at my right hand", since *this* God is
for the gnostics the evil God of the Jews, the Creator of
this evil world.[19] Absurd speculations? Not entirely, for
what is ultimately involved here is the conviction,
shared even today by many people, that *this* world is a
confused, chaotic, and largely negative product of lower
forces and that only the knowledge (gnosis) of this
nothingness can provide a way out of this.

While the "sitting at the right hand of God" indicates
for the gnostics that Christ has "bypassed" this God, the
Arians of the fourth century see it on the contrary as a
sign that the Son is *less* than the Father. *Eusebius of Caesarea*, the great Church historian who could never over-
come his closeness to Arianism, sees Christ, the Word
of God, as the "firstborn of the entire creation" (Col
1:15), as the first, unique *creature* of God, whom God

[19] Cf. Orbe, *Cristologia Gnostica*, 550–68. On the gnostic interpretation
of the "sitting at the right hand", cf. also Chapter 5 below, on reincarnation.

has made his fellow ruler "sharing his throne", to whom "alone among all the beings that have come into existence the honor was given of sitting at the right hand of the power and royal lordship of the Almighty".[20] It seems to be something unthinkable and unacceptable for Eusebius that this "sitting at the right hand of God" could be the expression of Christ's true divinity. For him, Christ remains a "being that has come into existence", the highest of all creatures, but not God in the substantial sense, for this would be incompatible for Eusebius with the uniqueness of God.

But are the defenders of the true divinity of Christ, consubstantial with the Father, correct to appeal to Psalm 110:1 ("The Lord said to my Lord, 'Sit at my right hand' ")? Is it not rather the case that it is only through the Resurrection that Christ "was exalted to the right hand of God" (Acts 2:33)? The Arians appeal to Acts 3:36 ("God has made him Lord and Messiah") to support their view that Christ is not substantially God, since he was only *made* Lord. Against this, *Athanasius of Alexandria* develops the view that has remained determinative for orthodox Christology: Christ is the Son of God and God, consubstantial with the Father. He reigns eternally with the Father, and this is why Psalm 110:1 also refers to his eternal lordship,[21] but the

---

[20] *Dem. ev.* v, 3 (Heikel 219, 21–34); cf. M.-J. Rondeau, "Le 'Commentaire des Psaumes' de Diodore de Tarse et l'exégèse antique du Psaume 109/110", *Revue de l'histoire des religions* 88/176 (1969), 5–33, 153–188; 89/117 (1970), 5–33.

[21] *Contra Arianos* II, 13.

fact that his lordship is first established and grows, that God *makes* him Lord and Messiah, is interpreted by Athanasius in terms of "salvation history": Christ, who is by nature Lord and eternal King, does not become "more" Lord in the moment in which he is sent out, nor does he begin to be Lord and King only then. Rather, it is then that he was made, according to the flesh, what he always is; and when redemption has been accomplished, he also becomes Lord of the living and the dead. For from now on, everything serves him, and it is precisely of this that David sings: "The Lord says to my Lord, 'Sit at my right hand, until I put your enemies as a footstool under your feet' " (Ps 110:1).[22]

Here we have a majestic panoramic view that takes in at one and the same time eternity and salvation history, the divinity of Christ and his humanity. The one who created us has also become our Redeemer through the Incarnation,[23] and his eternal lordship is extended to all men through his glorified humanity. But controversies broke out again precisely about this last perspective. Does not "until I put your enemies as a footstool under your feet" mean that Christ's lordship will cease once this has been carried out? Does not Paul say in this connection: "When everything has been made subordinate to him, then the Son too will make himself subordinate to the one who has made all things subordinate to him, so that God may be all in all" (1 Cor 15:28)?

[22] Ibid., 14, 138.
[23] Ibid., 138f.

Marcellus of Ancyra, a zealous defender of the Council of Nicaea and a friend of Athanasius, upheld the view that everything that is said about Christ's sitting at the right hand of God refers to Christ as a man and thus has validity only for the time of the Incarnation, which has a beginning and, according to Marcellus, an end too. For Marcellus, Christ's humanity has significance only in time, not in eternity. At the "end of time", it will lose its function and will no longer be needed. Marcellus indeed goes even further, and it is this that has caused his orthodoxy to be called into question: the eternal Word of God, the Logos, will himself in a certain sense be absorbed into the Father at the end, so that nothing else exists besides God alone.[24] This appears to call into question the existence of the Son himself as a Divine Person.

The view that Christ's humanity had only a temporary significance was also held by that powerful spiritual movement of the early Church that appealed to the great but controversial figure of *Origen*. The offensive idea that Christ's body should live forever, that his flesh should remain forever, forced Christian thinkers who were under the spell of Origen to swerve aside again and again into the realm of allegory. In the case of *Evagrius of Pontus*, the influential monastic theologian, the "sitting at the right hand of God" means simply that the preexistent spiritual soul of Christ is wholly "anointed

[24] On Marcellus, cf. A. Grillmeier, *Jesus der Christus*, 414–39.

with the knowledge of the unity . . . for the right hand, according to the interpretation of those who possess knowledge, means the monad and the unity".[25] The important point is this purely spiritual vision, devoid of images and concepts, of the primal divine unity, to which Christ leads us: his earthly body represents here at most a kind of "entrance door"—nothing more. "Bodiliness has no longer any meaning whatsoever for the reestablished world. It is the temporal form in which the Spirit-Christ appears for us. . . . Only the Spirit has meaning, and the only spiritual act that has meaning is knowledge." [26]

This "pneumatomonism" (the granting of validity exclusively to the spiritual) emerges once again in an exemplary fashion in the *iconoclastic conflict* of the Eastern Church, for the very concrete issue at stake in the pictorial representations of the *human* form of Christ is the extent to which we are permitted to hold on to the bodily form of Christ. Already *Eusebius of Caesarea* rejected images of Christ because Christ's human form had been wholly "swallowed up" by the glory of the divine form. Why should one continue to hold on to something that was only a transitional phase? The important thing *now* was to seek Christ "in his pure state", as the spiritual-heavenly Christ. In the same way, the Council of 754, which was hostile to images, requires a

---

[25] *Kephalaia gnostica* IV, 21 (PO 28, 145); cf. Grillmeier, *Jesus der Christus*, 561–68.

[26] Grillmeier, *Jesus der Christus*, 567.

spiritual adoration. It is not permissible to hold on to Christ, who is enthroned at the right hand of God, in the earthly, fleshly form that he has laid aside: "If anyone presumes to take hold with *material colors* of the divine form [*charaktēra*] of the incarnate Word of God, instead of venerating him with all his heart with *the eyes of the spirit*, where he sits on the throne of glory, more radiant than the sun, at the right hand of the Father, let him be anathema." [27] *Theodore Studites*, without doubt the most significant of the defenders of images, went to the very center of the Church's rule of faith to find a subtle answer to this spiritualization that was opposed to images. His monks are asking whether it is not a sign of imperfection to employ images, and whether it is not better to adore Christ in a purely spiritual, imageless way. The Abbot of Studius makes a wonderful reply: "Thus if anyone should say, 'Since I ought to venerate Christ spiritually, it is superfluous to venerate him in his icon', then he should know that thereby he denies also the spiritual veneration of Christ. For if he does not see with his spirit Christ sitting in *human* form at the right hand of the Father, then he does not venerate him at all. On the contrary, he denies that the Word has become flesh. Against this, his icon is the reliable witness that the eternal Word has taken the form of man." [28] If contemplation and the prayer of the Christian are to

[27] Mansi 13, 336 E; on this, cf. my book *God's Human Face: The Christ-Icon* (San Francisco: Ignatius Press, 1994), 160.

[28] PG 99, 1288 CD.

reach Christ in his reality, this cannot involve anything other than a spiritual vision of his transfigured *humanity*, in which he lives "at the right hand of the Father". The words with which Bishop *Cyril of Jerusalem* appeals to the catechumens at the beginning of his catecheses show how deeply this conviction is rooted in the early Church's rule of faith: "Lift up now the gaze of the spirit: picture now to yourselves in the spirit the choirs of angels, God, the Lord of the universe, on his throne, his only begotten Son at his right hand, and the Spirit beside them." [29]

Now we leap across many centuries. The question whether one is permitted during such contemplation to picture Christ to oneself as a man exercised *Teresa of Avila* greatly. The path that she found here reminds us strongly of the teaching that Theodore Studites gave his monks. Teresa relates in her autobiography that she was much unsettled by certain authors whom she was instructed to read, because they counseled that one should endeavor to transcend all bodily images, "not even excluding those of the humanity of Christ", because they were a hindrance to contemplation. Teresa could not grasp how turning away from the humanity of Christ could be taught as a path of the spiritual life; those who teach in this manner "quote what the Lord said to the apostles when he [promised them] the coming of the Holy Spirit, that is to say, when he ascended to heaven (cf. Jn 16:7). But I maintain that the visible

[29] *Procatechesis*, no. 15.

presence of the Lord would not have been any hindrance to the apostles if they had had the faith that they
had after the descent of the Holy Spirit, viz., the faith
that Christ is both man and God." [30] No, the visible reality of the Lord could not be any hindrance to prayer.
It is fascinating how Teresa describes her discovery of
the vision of the humanity of Christ. She followed only
for a short time the false path of the allegedly "spiritual"
contemplation that holds even the Incarnation of God
to be too inferior a stage. Teresa is drawn back powerfully to the humanity of Christ, and she receives visions
that confirm her on this path: indescribable light, unutterable beauty. She is permitted to see Christ, his hands,
his face, his whole form: "The Lord almost always
showed himself to me *in the form of his Resurrection*, and
this is also how I saw him in the Host. It was only
when he wanted to strengthen me in some tribulation
that he showed me a few times his wounds. Sometimes,
though more seldom, he appeared to me on the Cross
or as he was in the Garden of Olives, or with the
crown of thorns, or as he bore the Cross. He showed
himself in this way to me when he wanted to console
me and other persons in tribulations, *but he always appeared to me* with a *transfigured* body." [31] If one wishes to
call these appearances an "image", "then it is a *living*

[30] *Vida*, chap. 22, 1. Like these Catholic authors of whom Teresa
speaks, Calvin too will appeal to John 16:7 ("It is better for you that I depart . . .") in order to reject the search for the bodily presence of Christ
(Eucharist, image): cf. nn. 35–37 below.

[31] *Vida*, chap. 29, 4.

image: it is not a dead man but the living Christ, who reveals himself at one and the same time as man and God, not as he lay in the tomb but as he came out from there after the Resurrection. But sometimes the Lord appears in such great majesty that one cannot in the least doubt that it is he himself. This happens especially at Communion; for then we know already in any case that he is present, since the Faith teaches us this." [32]

Here we have a wonderful expression, in living plenitude, of the mystery of our credal article: Christ, "*as he is himself*", "*the living Christ*", man and God, the risen, transfigured Body that faith receives in the bread of life, in Communion: Teresa knows that the entire sacramental dimension of the Church stands and falls with the abiding, transfigured humanity of Christ. She knows that the Risen One is now near us in the Sacrament. [33]

A contemporary of Teresa, in many respects at the antipodes to her, shows us how closely the mystery of Christ is linked with that of the Church precisely in the article of faith, "He sits at the right hand of the Father." *John Calvin* emphasizes again and again that Christ ascended *bodily* into heaven and that he is now there, not here: he sits *there* at the right hand of the Father; even if the philosophers do not like this, the Holy Spirit teaches it. But this means for Calvin that he is no longer with us bodily in any way at all. We do indeed

[32] *Vida*, chap. 28, 7.
[33] *Vida*, chap 22, 6.

always have Christ with us, but not his fleshly presence, only the presence of his majesty, of his Holy Spirit;[34] bodily, he is *only* in heaven. But this means for Calvin, further, that he cannot be *bodily* in the bread and wine of the Eucharist and that he cannot be portrayed bodily on earth. "We do not have fellowship with God through an image or through any other earthly object that we choose for ourselves, not even through the visible elements of the Lord's Supper, but only through the Holy Spirit, who has no difficulty in uniting what is separated in space." [35] Calvin wants to emphasize the real, bodily glorification of Christ, but for him, this excludes the possibility that "Jesus Christ dwells in the bread" (of the Eucharist), since otherwise Christ would have to leave heaven; in order to have Christ present, the working of the Holy Spirit, which unites us to Christ, is sufficient.[36] It is only consistent when Calvin rejects the image of Christ just as much as the *bodily* presence of the Lord in the Eucharist.

Other Reformers too quote this credal article against the real presence of Christ in the Eucharist: *Oecolampadius* and *Zwingli* deduce from this that Christ could not be simultaneously bodily on the altar and in heaven. This means that the Lord's Supper is only a memorial

[34] *Inst. chrét.* II, 16, 14 and IV, 17, 26.

[35] Margarete Stirm, *Die Bilderfrage in der Reformation* (Gütersloh, 1977) (QFRG vol. 45), 212f., referring to the *Opera Selecta* (Barth-Niesel) II, 131.

[36] *Inst. chrét.* IV, 17, 31.

celebration.[37] *Luther* discusses in detail the "sitting at the right hand of the Father" in his polemical works. He accuses the "enthusiasts" of having a childish idea of the "right hand" of God, as if Christ sat on a golden throne there. In reality, no place is meant here, but rather "the omnipotent power of God, which at one and the same time can be nowhere and yet in all places".[38] Luther, of course, goes too far in the opposite direction when he proceeds to deduce from this the omnipresence of the Body of Christ: "Wherever the right hand of God is, there must the Body and Blood of Christ be." [39] Without discussing the problems of Luther's "doctrine of ubiquity", we can affirm that he absolutely follows the line of the early Church's rule of faith when he sees not an antithesis (like Calvin and Zwingli) between the "sitting at the right hand" and the presence in the Lord's Supper but rather a profound connection. The fact that Christ is enthroned at the right hand of the Father is seen precisely in his living, bodily presence in the Eucharist.

3. The Mystery of His Present Lordship

"Between the last mystery of the life of Christ, which lies in the past, namely, the Ascension, and the mystery that we still await, namely, the parousia, there exists

---

[37] On this and what follows, cf. M. Lienhard, *Martin Luthers christologisches Zeugnis* (Berlin, 1980), esp. 146–84.

[38] WA 23, 133, 19.

[39] WA 23, 143, 32.

one mystery that is contemporary with ourselves: the fact that Christ sits at the Father's right." [40] This article of faith is in a sense the most ecclesiological of the christological articles. The brief glimpses of the history of the exposition of this article have repeatedly made clear the ecclesiological component. This is not surprising, since what is at issue here is precisely the *present-day* relationship of Christ to his Church. No Father of the Church emphasized this aspect of our article of faith as strongly as *Augustine*. We shall therefore conclude by quoting some texts from his abundant writings on this subject.

> Your faith, beloved, is clear about this, and we know that this is how you have learned it from the instruction of the heavenly teacher on whom you have set your hope: that our Lord Jesus Christ, who suffered for us and rose again, is the Head of the Church, and that the Church is his Body.... Since therefore he is the Head of the Church and the Church is his Body, the entire Christ is Head and Body together. The Head has already risen: thus, we bear our Head in heaven. Our Head makes intercession for us. Our sinless, deathless Head already pleads with God for our sins, so that we too, when we rise again at the end and are transformed into heavenly glory, may follow after our Head. For where the Head is, there must the other members be too. . . . Brothers, see the love of our Head. He is already in heaven, and yet he suffers here below, as long as

[40] J. Daniélou, *Etudes d'exégèse judéo-chrétienne* (Paris, 1966), in the chapter "La session à la droite du Père", 42–48, at 48.

the Church here below suffers. Christ hungers here below; he thirsts here below; he is naked, a stranger, sick, in prison. For he says that whatever his Body suffers here, he too suffers (cf. Mt 25:42–45).[41]

Since our Lord Jesus Christ wished to ascend to heaven on the fortieth day, he recommended his Body where it lay. For he saw in advance that many would honor him, because he ascended to heaven, but that the honors they displayed would be meaningless, because at the same time they oppressed his members on earth. . . . From on high, he called to Saul the persecutor: "Saul, Saul, why are you persecuting me?" (Acts 9:4). I ascended to heaven, but still I am lying on the earth; here I sit at the right hand of the Father, there I am still hungry, thirsty, and a stranger! . . . See, there I am lying, I who am now ascending on high! For I ascend because I am the Head, but my Body is still lying there! Take care: do not strike it. Take care: do not harm it. Take care: do not trample on it![42]

"God sits upon his holy throne" (Ps 47:9). What is his holy throne? Surely, it is heaven. For as we know, Christ has ascended into heaven with the body with which he was crucified, and he sits at the right hand of the Father; we also expect him to come thence to judge the living and the dead. Thus the heavens are his holy throne. Do you too want to be his throne? Do not imagine that you could not be his throne: prepare a place for him in your heart, and he will be happy to sit on his throne there. For he is assuredly the power of God and the wisdom of God. And what does Scripture say about Wisdom itself? "The

[41] *Sermo* CXXXVII, I–II; PL 38, 754f.
[42] *In Ep. Ioa. Tract.* x, 5, 9; PL 35, 2060f.

soul of the righteous is a throne of wisdom" (Wis 7). Accordingly, if the soul of the righteous is the throne of wisdom, and your soul is righteous, then you will be the royal throne of Wisdom.[43]

These two perspectives complement each other in Augustine: since the individual, the soul, is always also Church and Bride, what is said about the Church holds good of the individual too. The indicator for faith in the bodily glorification of the risen Jesus is, for Augustine, love for his Body, the Church. Where love for his Body, especially in the poorest of his members, is alive, then that exchange of which already Paul speaks is rightly present: not only does the Head suffer with the members, but the members too have already been raised up with Christ and indeed share his throne at the right hand of God (cf. Eph 2:1–6). In patristic theology, our glorification together with Christ is often called our "deification".[44] Let *John Chrysostom* give us the final word here, wholly in the perspective sketched by Augustine:

And how ought one to conceive of this, that he has raised us up together with him? For no one has yet been raised up, except in the sense *that we are risen because the Head has risen*. It was in this way that God gave us a share in his throne. For if the Head is on the throne, then the Body too is on the throne. This is why Paul adds: "in Christ

43 *En. in Ps.* XLVI, 10; PL 36, 529f.
44 See Chapter 2 below.

Jesus". . . . The sitting at the right hand is the greatest honor, with nothing to equal it. This statement holds true of us also: we too are to sit with him on thrones. This is truly an overflowing richness. Truly, exceedingly great is his power, that he lets us sit on the throne together with Christ. And if you had a thousand lives, would you not lay them down for the sake of Christ? If you were to be thrown into the fire, would you not accept that willingly? Again he says: "I will that they be with me, where I am" (Jn 17:24). Even if we were to be torn to pieces every day, would we not be glad to bear this for the sake of the promise? Think of where Christ sits on his throne! "Above all principalities and powers!" And with whom are you to sit on the throne? With him! And who are you? By nature a dead man, a child of wrath. And what good things have you done? Nothing (cf. Eph 2:1–3)! Then it is truly time to cry out: "O depth of the riches, the wisdom and the knowledge of God!" (Rom 11:33).[45]

---

[45] *Hom. in Ep. ad Eph.* IV, 2; PG 62, 32f.; cf. *In Gen. sermo* II, 1; PG 54, 587f.: "For God did not cease to do and to undertake everything, until he brought man on high and gave him a place at his right hand; Paul too tells us this: 'He has raised us up with him and given us a place at his right hand in heaven in Christ Jesus' (Eph 2:6)."

Chapter II

IS MAN TO BECOME GOD?
ON THE MEANING OF THE CHRISTIAN
DOCTRINE OF DEIFICATION

The Greek Fathers often said that the Son of God became a man on earth so that man might enter the
sphere of God. The statement "God made himself a
man in order that man might be able to become God" [1]
was one of the most influential formulations of the
Christian message in that period. To become God, to
be deified: this seemed to be the highest goal of all
human yearnings. Saint Basil indeed can state this as a
conviction with which his contemporaries were familiar: "The summit of all that can be wished: to become
God".[2]

[1] Athanasius, *Inc.* LIV, 3; PG 25, 192 B; cf. *Ar.* I, 38,; PG 26, 92 B; the
formulation is found in one or other form in all the Church Fathers, in
the Middle Ages, and into the modern period. Further references are to
be found in my more extensive study "Über die richtige Fassung des
dogmatischen Begriffs der Vergöttlichung des Menschen", in *FZPhTh* 34
(1987), 3–47.

[2] Basil, *Spir.* IX, 23; PG 32, 109 C = SC 17f., p. 329; cf. *Contra Eunomium* II, 3, 5 and 4; PG 29, 580 B and 665 B.

Such a wish seems no longer to exist in our period of history, at least if one believes those who assert that the idea of deification was typically "hellenistic", the massive invasion of a tendency that was utterly foreign to the original Christianity. Adolf von Harnack and other Church historians of his school saw in the doctrine of deification "the most striking proof of a hellenization of Christianity that achieved control, thereby doing harm to the religious moralism preached by Jesus".[3] A number of contemporary authors continue to see things in this way, adding that "modern man" aims much more at the "humanization of man" than at his deification.[4] Other theologians reject the idea of deification on purely religious grounds: the finitude of man, the fact that he is not God, constitutes his otherness vis-à-vis God, which was the Creator's intention in the very act of creating him, and is something that man is not at all permitted to transcend in the direction of becoming God.[5] Others object that expressions like "deification" or "becoming God" remain ambiguous, are unbiblical, cause only confusion, etc.

Under such circumstances, should one continue at all to speak of deification? Would it not be better wholly to avoid such disputed expressions, so open to attack? In order to reply to this, one must first give the question its true meaning: What are we speaking of here? Is

[3] J. Gross, *La divinisation du chrétien d'après les Pères Grecs* (Paris, 1938), 4.

[4] Thus Hans Küng in *Christsein* (Munich, 1975), 433.

[5] Cf. J. Pohier, *Quand je dis Dieu* (Paris, 1977).

it certain that the criticism of the concepts does not attack something that belongs to the essence of the Christian Faith?

In what follows, accordingly, we shall briefly investigate first: What meaning did the Church Fathers attribute to the concept of deification? In the second section, we shall deal with some views that are incompatible with the Christian Faith in order to draw thence in the third section some practical consequences for the proclamation of the Christian Faith.

1. The Christian Meaning of Deification

On the threshold of the modern period, a young genius, Pico della Mirandola, sketched the essential outlines of an image of man that is wholly ordered to deification. In his famous discourse on the dignity of man, he has God address his creature as follows:

O Adam, we have not bestowed on you one particular dwelling place, or one particular countenance, or any special gift, so that you may create for yourself every dwelling place, every outward appearance, and every gift that you wish for yourself. The rest of the creatures are determined according to the laws of their nature, which we have prescribed; they are kept within their boundaries by these. But you are not limited by any boundary: rather, you are to establish your own nature through your own free will, upon which I have made your destiny in life depend. I have placed you in the center of the world, so that you may look around you comfortably from this position at all that exists in the world. We have not created you as a heavenly being or as an earthly being, neither as mortal nor as immortal, in order that you, as the Lord of your own self, may be endowed with the honor and the duty of modeling your own being, in which you choose to live. You are free to be perverted into subhuman forms, but you are equally free to be reborn in higher divine forms through your own decision.[6]

This text is not in the least the expression of a humanistic concept of the Superman or of the idea that human freedom is the creation of one's own self: rather, it presupposes the classical line of patristic tradition— man, created in the image of God, is endowed with a freedom, in virtue of which he is able to become what he has chosen to be; but his only choice is either to sink below his human dignity or to transcend himself through a divine rebirth.

More than a millennium before Pico, Hippolytus of Rome had already sketched this image of man in very similar phrases:

After this, he created out of all the substances the lord of all things; he did not want to create a god or an angel, in order not to make any mistake, but—I do not wish to lead anyone astray—a man. For if he had wanted to make you a god, he could have done this, as we can see in the exam-

---

[6] *Die Würde des Menschen* (Fribourg, Frankfurt, and Vienna: Pantheon-Verlag, n.d.), 52; cf. H. de Lubac's commentary in *Pic de la Mirandole* (Paris, 1977).

ple of the Logos. He wanted to have you as a man, and he created you as such. But if you too want to be God, then listen to the one who created you and do not resist him here below, in order that, when you have been found to be faithful in small things, you may also be able to receive what is great.[7]

Man is truly created as man and thus is *willed* to be such: he is not a god unaware of himself, as the gnosis of all epochs supposes. But if he wills, he can become God, by putting into practice the true meaning of his human existence: indeed, he does not possess any other way to become truly man. This formulation appears more than a little paradoxical. In order to be sure that this is not merely a play on words, we must verify the formula "christologically".

a. *Christ as the "Humanized" God and "Deified" Man*

The Christian Faith affirms that Christ is true God and true man, without commixture and without separation (Council of Chalcedon). When the Church spoke of deification, this was possible only through a reference to the mystery of Christ: What does "true man" mean, if one asserts at the same time that Christ always was and remained God?[8] Modern Christology, above all Protestant Christology, is determined by great anxiety

[7] *Philosophoumena* X, 33; PG 16, 3450 B.
[8] J. Pelikan, *The Christian Tradition. A History of the Development of Doctrine*, I, 155.

to preserve the full humanity of Christ. It fears that if one follows the ancient tradition in speaking of deification, the *true* humanity will be reduced or even altogether dissolved. This is why many reject classical Christology, which is taken to be incapable of giving an account of the true humanity of Christ,[9] and this then leads to the denial of the deification of man.

In order to interpret correctly the Fathers' teaching on deification,[10] one must begin from its *soteriological* aspect. Man's true salvation consists in his being given the closest possible resemblance and configuration to God. Thanks to the working of Christ and of the Holy Spirit, man begins to attain this resemblance.

For Athanasius, as for the other Fathers who engage in the struggle against Arianism, the deification of man is one of the chief arguments for the divinity of Christ and, at a somewhat later date, for the divinity of the Holy Spirit.

> The Logos does not in the least belong among the created things: rather, he is their Creator. This is why he took on a created and human body, in order to renew it as its Creator and *to deify it in himself* and thus to lead us all with him into the kingdom of heaven, in keeping with the resemblance we are given to *him*. Since he united himself to

[9] Cf. my study "'Aporie der Zweinaturenlehre': Überlegungen zur Christologie von Wolfhart Pannenberg", in *FZPhTh* 24 (1977), 428–45.

[10] H. Merki has investigated the Greek sources and Christian transformations of this theme: *Omoiôsis Theô. Von der platonischen Angleichung an Gott zur Gottähnlichkeit bei Gregor von Nyssa* (Fribourg, 1952).

a creature, man would not have been deified anew had not the Son been true God. Man would not have come closer to the Father unless the One who assumed a human body had been the natural and true Logos of the Father. And just as we would not have been freed from sin and the curse if the flesh taken on by the Logos had not been a human flesh in terms of its nature—since we have nothing in common with an alien being—even so man would not have been *deified* had not the incarnate One been begotten of the Father as his own true Logos. For this reason, the unification (*sunaphê*) took place in this way, so that the human nature would be united to the divine, thus ensuring its salvation and its deification.[11]

With the clear statement that only God can deify (and that for this reason the Son and the Spirit are God), the Fathers explain at the same time that the deification can never be a self-deification on the part of man. The entire tradition agrees in affirming that deification takes place only "through grace";[12] in keep-

[11] Athanasius, *Ar.* I, 70; PG 26, 296 AB. Gregory Nazianzen brings out in the same way the divinity of the Holy Spirit: "Indeed, if the Spirit is not to be adored, how then does he deify me in baptism? And if he is to be adored, is he not then worthy of worship? And if he is worthy of worship, how is he then not God? One follows on from the other, truly a golden chain of salvation. And it is from the Spirit that we receive rebirth; from this rebirth comes the reinstatement in our first condition; and from this reinstatement comes the knowledge of the one who has reestablished us": *Or.* XXXI, 28; SC 250, 35.

[12] We mention only a few examples from the countless texts: Basil, *Contra Eunomium* III, 5; PG 29, 665 BC; Sophronius of Jerusalem, PG 87, 328 BC; Augustine: *Ex gratia sua deificatos, non de substantia sua natos*: PL 36, 565.

ing with this, one reads often that grace is "deifying" by
its very nature.[13] But even if all deification is understood unambiguously as grace, nevertheless it remains
the true goal for which man has been created.[14]

b. *In What Does Deification Consist?*

Maximus the Confessor specifies as clearly as possible
the substance of our deification: "The one deified
through grace receives for himself *everything* that God
possesses, apart from the identify of substance." [15] Everything: this could look like a rhetorical exaggeration. And
yet, this is precisely what the entire Western and Eastern
tradition wanted to say when it spoke of the grace of
deification: the one who is counted worthy of the deifying grace does not receive "a part" or "something" of
God but truly God as a whole. Thus the Fathers understand participation in the divine life as the goal of our
existence.[16]

Man can become *everything* that God is, apart from the
identity of substance, for he is created in view of such a
participation. To be created in the image and likeness of
God means that one has been designed and "produced"
in view of an ever more perfect configuration to God.

---

[13] Gregory Palamas, *Triad.* 3, 1, ed. Meyendorff, 625.

[14] Maximus the Confessor, *Qu. Thal.* 60; PG 90, 621 A.

[15] *Amb. Io.* 41; PG 91, 1308.

[16] Cf., e.g., Cyril of Alexandria, PG 72, 908 D – 909 A; 74, 192 AB; 75,
968 CD.

This permits us to see that the deification through grace does not in the least denote that human nature is dissolved: on the contrary, it denotes the inmost realization of this nature.

To become everything that God is, through grace and not through nature, means in concrete terms, according to a phrase of John Damascene, that "through participation in God, man becomes by grace what Christ is by nature".[17] Christian deification is no abstract, anonymous deification: in its concrete realization, it is what Paul calls the "adoption as children" (*huiothesia*). *Theopoiêsis* is concretely *huiopoiêsis*,[18] becoming sons by grace in and through the one who is Son by nature:[19] this is the meaning of the formula so often used by the Fathers and also by the subsequent tradition: we become gods and sons through designation (*thêsei*) and not through nature (*phusei*), through grace and not through nature.[20]

c. *Redemption and Deification in Christ*

"Christ did not come to change or to transform human nature, but in order to lead it to where it was before the

---

[17] John Damascene, *Fid. orth.* IV; PG 94, 1164 B.

[18] Athanasius, *Ep. Serap.* I, 25; PG 26, 589 B.

[19] Athanasius, *Ar.* II, 59; PG 26, 273.

[20] Athanasius, *Ar.* II, 59; PG 26, 272 C; numerous texts; cf. the article *thêsis* in G. W. H. Lampe's *Patristic Greek Lexicon*; E. H. Kantorowicz, "*Deus per naturam, deus per gratium*: A Note on Mediaeval Political Theology", in *Harv. Theol. Rev.* 45 (1952), 253–77.

fall, to immortality." [21] Thus deification is nothing other than true "humanization", the reestablishing of man in his original dignity. In line with Pico and Hippolytus, Maximus locates the reestablishing of man above all in an act of the will: "If Adam willingly listened to the seducer, if he looked and ate with his will, then it is primarily the will in us that has suffered damage. If this is so, and if the Logos had not assumed the will in his Incarnation, as they [the Monothelites] assert, then I have not got free from sin, and thus I am not redeemed either, for that which was not assumed [by Christ] has not been redeemed." [22]

Deification is located in the reestablishing of fallen man in his innate dignity. If it is clear that the fall was caused by a perversion of the human will, then it follows that the reestablishing must affect above all the act of human willing. "For the glorious God became man, not in order to deceive the imagination of his creature, but in order to destroy definitively, through participation in our nature, the tendency [to evil] that was sown by the serpent. The Incarnation of the Logos has changed the fundamental attitude [*hexis*], not the nature, so that we might cease to be accustomed to remember evil and might clothe ourselves in the love of God—not changed into something that we had not

---

[21] Methodius of Olympus, *De res.* 1, 49; ed. Bonwetsch 303, 6–8.
[22] *Pyrrh.*; PG 91, 325 A.

been before, but gloriously renewed through being changed into what we once were." [23]

Creation and redemption correspond to one another. Deification dissolves not the work of the Creator but the work of the tempter. Deified humanity is precisely that humanity which has attained the goal of its creation. This humanity, new because renewed and fully realized, is the humanity of the incarnate Word, in which, according to Maximus, the entire *new man* is included. In the mode of existence (*tropos tês huparxeôs*) of the *incarnate* Word, we are able to see what a *deified humanity* is. Because Christ carried out the salvific design of the Father as a man, endowed with a human will, a human heart, and human hands (cf. Vatican II, *Gaudium et Spes*, no. 22), he reveals in the characteristics of his own mode of human existence the face of the deified man.

d. *Deification of Man through the Sacraments of the Church*

The only path to deification consists in the ever deeper configuration to Christ. To become "sons in the Son": it is in this that deification consists. According to Nicholas Cabasilas (ca. 1320–63), the great Byzantine "lay theologian", this configuration takes place only through "life in Christ", the "internal unification with Christ".[24] But the entrances through which we attain to this life

[23] Diadochus of Photice, *Ascens.* VI; SC 5f., 168; PG 65, 1145 D – 1148 A.

[24] *Life in Christ* II; PG 150, 521 A.

are the "mysteries", the sacraments of Christ, through
which our life is configured to his. "All those who imi-
tate his death through symbolic acts, as it were copying
this death that he suffered for us, are renewed by Christ
thanks to the realities (indicated in the symbols). Christ
creates them anew and makes them sharers in his own
life." In the holy mysteries, we trace the image (so to
speak) of the burial of Christ and proclaim his death.
Thereby, we are born anew and are configured super-
naturally to the Redeemer. "For in them, we live and
move and have our being", as Paul says (Acts 17:28).[25]
The mysteries are the "gates of righteousness" through
which heaven bends down to us and God comes to
meet us; in them, the Christian (thanks to a somewhat
free but profound exegesis) finds his "living space":
through baptism he finds being, through the myron
(the anointing of confirmation) he finds movement, and
through the Eucharist he finds life.[26] Such an existence
in the mysteries already forms the new man and permits
him to acquire even here below the senses that can taste
and *experience* the divine life. Cabasilas reminds us that if
we should fail to develop already in our earthly life organs and senses that can grasp the hidden life of God in
us, then we would be unable to possess this in the future life.[27] The deified man is born in the womb of existence here on earth.

[25] Ibid., I, 501 D.
[26] Ibid., I, 504 AC.
[27] Ibid., I, 493 B – 496 B.

The view of the early Church was in keeping with this too. It is astonishing to see how emphatically a Clement of Alexandria insists on the fact that the one baptized is already perfect, already deified.

> Through baptism we are illuminated, through illumination we have received adoption as children, through adoption as children we are perfected, through perfection we are made immortal. "You are gods, and all of you sons of the Most High" (Ps 81:6). But this event is given various names: gift of grace, illumination, perfection, bath. "Bath", since it is clear that our sins are washed away; "gift of grace", since thereby the penalties for our trespasses are remitted; "illumination", since thereby that sacred light of redemption is seen, i.e., since we see the Deity clearly; and we give the name "perfection" to that which lacks nothing. For what is still lacking to the one who has come to know God? For it would be truly unthinkable that something imperfect could be called God's "gift of grace"; since he is perfect, assuredly he gives only perfect gifts.[28]

The baptized *is* a perfect being, a "new creation" (2 Cor 5:17). He is deified. Is this to be an automatic process? Does not this idea of a deification through the sacraments expose itself to the famous criticism of Harnack, who saw salvation reduced here to a "pharmacological process" in which the physical automatism of redemption excludes the ethical dimension?[29]

[28] *Paed.* I, chap. 5, 26; SC 70, 159–61.
[29] *Das Wesen des Christentums*, Akademie edn. Leipzig, 145–47.

In order to get an idea of how the Fathers conceived of our cooperation, let us listen to a subtle text from Diadochus of Photice. The Fathers were aware that this cooperation could never do anything other than follow on God's free initiative, but must on the other hand precede the graced perfecting of his work in us.

Sacred grace gives us two good things through the baptism of rebirth, one of which infinitely surpasses the other. The one is given us immediately; for grace itself creates us anew in the water and brings all the marks of the soul to shine, i.e., what is in accordance with the image of God, after it has smoothed out all the wrinkles of our sin (cf. Eph 5:27). But grace waits with the other gift, in order as it were to realize it together with ourselves; this is what corresponds to the resemblance.

When the spirit now begins fully to taste the good things of the Holy Spirit, then we must know that now grace begins to portray the resemblance upon that which is in accordance with the image. But as the painters first portray the image of a man in one color and gradually let it shine through one further color and then yet another color, thus ensuring the resemblance of what is portrayed down to the last hair, just so does God's grace first begin to reestablish through baptism the image that man was when he was created. When grace observes that we yearn with all our force for the beauty of the resemblance and stand naked and modest in her workshop, then she lets virtue upon virtue shine forth, so that the beauty of the soul rises up from glory to glory, thus creating for the soul the quality of resemblance.

The inner sense then reveals to us that we are taking on the form of resemblance. But we recognize from the illumination that the resemblance is perfected. For the spirit receives all the virtues through its sense, by striding onwards in a determined measure and an unutterable rhythm. But no one can acquire spiritual love unless he is illuminated by the Holy Spirit in all fullness. . . . For just as the whole fullness of the colors that are painted on the image holds fast on the copies the resemblance to what is portrayed, down to the very smile on the face, so is it with whose who have been painted by the divine grace in the resemblance to God. Here the illumination makes it clear through the love, which now comes, that that which was created according to the image has now come completely to the splendor of the resemblance. For freedom from passion cannot be bestowed on the soul by any other virtue than love alone. "For love is the fullness of the law" (Rom 13:10). In this way, our inner man is renewed from day to day in savoring love and finds his fullness in love's perfection.[30]

This text most effectively unites the various aspects of deification: the exalted state of the gift—namely, the renewed image—demands our cooperation and stimulates it—the image is to become resemblance—in order finally to transcend it through the perfect gift of love.

The patristic statements about the priest as a deified and deifying man can be understood in the same perspective. Let us mention one good example: the great

---

[30] *Cent.* c. 89.

discourse by the young Gregory Nazianzen on the priesthood. The exaltedness of his new task makes the one who is about to become a priest shudder, causing him to shrink in terror from receiving ordination: "One must first purify oneself before one purifies others; one must be formed before one forms others; one must become light in order to illuminate; one must draw close to God in order to bring the others close to him; one must be sanctified in order to sanctify, to lead others by the hand and counsel them with prudence." Here is the greatness of the priesthood: the priest is "the defender of the truth, who stands together with the angels, gives glory together with the archangels, sends up the sacrificial gift to the heavenly altar, shares the priestly office with Christ, models anew the creative clay, bringing forth from this the image [of God], preparing it for the world above, and—more than all this—the priest becomes God and deifies others." [31]

The vocation to the Christian life, and in a particular way to the priestly office, opens up here onto dimensions that transcend our concepts: by "becoming God" we are to make others gods.

2. Man's Self-Deification and Self-Destruction

The Fathers were able to proclaim this unheard-of vocation of man because they knew that this is possible only

[31] *Or.* II, 71 and 73; PG 35, 480 B – 481 B; SC 274, 185–87.

within the "wonderful exchange" between God and man, God's "humanization" and man's "deification", an exchange that only the divine love is able to carry out. Maximus has formulated this in a marvelous fashion: "It is said that God and man served one another mutually as models: God humanizes himself for man through his love for him, to the same extent to which man, strengthened by love, deifies himself for God; man is caught up in rapture by God to the Unknown, in the Spirit, to the same extent as he reveals, through his virtues, the God who is by nature invisible." [32]

Maximus sees in love that power that brings it about that man incarnates God in a life that is in keeping with Christ. And it is precisely in this way that love deifies him in accordance with the example given by God, who has incarnated himself out of love for man, to the point even of laying down his own life. Thus, the path of deification can be no other path than that of an incarnation of God's love in our life.[33]

Now, however, if we wish to speak of deification, things look unavoidably different to us: the idea that we "are caught up in rapture by God to the Unknown" precisely on the path of *kenôsis*, the loving gift of one's self, is the crass antithesis of what modern psychology would call our vain dream of deification. The biblical text calls "becoming like God" man's oldest temptation.

[32] *Amb. Io.* 10; PG 91, 1113 BC.

[33] We have here the beautiful idea of the continuing incarnation of the Word in the human virtues; cf. Maximus, *Amb. Io.* 7; PG 91, 1084 D.

But the God whom man wants to resemble—without God, however, only through man himself—this imaginary god is not in the least the One who has made himself known as the God of Abraham, Isaac, and Jacob, as the Father of Jesus Christ. He is a hallucinatory projection who locks man up in a demonic circle that lies between an imaginary omnipotence of this God and the powerlessness that man hates, the powerlessness from which he dreams that he will be set free.

One is tempted to set up a kind of typology of the forms of human self-deification, as these have been thought out. The sketch we offer here makes no claims to completeness, but it can offer a stimulus to investigate more precisely those forms of deification that do not correspond to the Christian Faith.

We can distinguish between two great forms outside Christianity. Their characteristics can be discerned through the different ways in which they interpret the Delphic inscription *gnôthi seauton*, "Know thyself."

a. The first form can be called the *gnostic* interpretation. "Know thyself" would mean here: know your true self, discover that in keeping with your divine nature; you are a god who does not know about himself. This, roughly speaking, is the answer given by all gnostic tendencies, ancient and modern; gnosis "is self-knowledge, because one is a divine being from birth onward".[34] The path of deification is in principle no

---

[34] A. J. Festugière, *Hermétisme et mystique païenne* (Paris, 1967), 58.

other path than that of knowledge itself. [35] To be precise, one should not speak of deification at all here, since man merely discovers what he already always *is*.

It is not possible for us to list in individual detail here how many forms of self-deification belong to this trend. Many authors have not hesitated to demonstrate the existence of a gnostic element in Hegel's thought,[36] and this is equally true of the thought of Marx.[37] The "divine man" is omnipresent in the modern systems of thought and ideologies, beginning with the cult of the genius [38] and going to the collective deification of the people, the nation, the "collective Prometheus".

b. The second form is the opposite of the first: "Know thyself" means here: you are no god, you are a mere man and nothing more! We can call this form the path of "radical finitude". Its characteristic is the rejection of all striving for deification. But why then should we regard it as a form of self-deification when it appears to be the opposite of this? It is the opposite at first sight, perhaps. For it is certain that the foreground is occupied

[35] Cf., e.g., the Hermetic tractate Poimandres no. 26; ed. Nock-Festugière, *Corpus Hermeticum* I, 16, 12f.

[36] This position was taken as early as 1835 by F. C. Baur, *Die christliche Gnosis*.

[37] This is maintained, for example, by L. Kolakowski in his monumental work *Hauptströmungen des Marxismus* (3 vols.); cf. already H. Heine, who warned against Marx and others as "godless self-deifiers"; W. Hädecke, *Heinrich Heine. Eine Biographie* (Munich, 1985).

[38] Cf., e.g., T. Carlyle, *On Heroes and Hero-Worship* (1840), who describes the hero as a divine being who transcends the limitations of mortal men.

at first by sensitivity to man's limits, his finitude and contingency. In the face of the threats, indeed the catastrophes produced by the titanism of self-deification, there is a plausibility to the warning that one must limit oneself to the human measure and not go beyond this.

But this path too turns soon enough into self-deification, though it does so more craftily than the first path; for where the limitation to radical finitude forbids in principle every yearning for the infinite and every transcendence, it soon ends by absolutizing finitude. This "pathos of finitude" [39] becomes a deification of contingency, which is equated with the absolute.[40] Gabriel Marcel saw in this attitude of radical finitude an "arrogance that blasphemes against God" rather than an "exaggerated humility":[41] the man who posits himself as radically finite posits himself thereby as unconditionally autonomous.[42]

One thing is common to both paths of self-deification, something that distinguishes them at the same time from the Christian path: they know of no fellowship between God and man. Man wants to be God and to possess what is divine without God. He wants to have this for himself. And he finds what he seeks: he becomes his own unique, absolute god. But

[39] F.-J. von Rintelen, *Philosophie der Endlichkeit* (1951), 40.

[40] This is how H. U. von Balthasar characterizes Heidegger's thought in *Apokalypse der deutschen Seele* (1938), III, 260.

[41] *Homo Viator* (1944), 83.

[42] Cf. W. Dilthey, *Gesammelte Schriften* VII (Leipzig, 1927), 290.

since he is *nothing* through his own self, since he has received everything, what he deifies is his own nothingness, and the murderous countenance of all self-deification discloses itself in this closed, hellish loneliness: self-deification is the self-destruction of man.[43]

3. "Humanization" through "Deification"

In *L'Etre et le Néant*, Jean-Paul Sartre says: "Human existence means striving to be God; or, if one wills, one can put it this way: man is ultimately a yearning to be God."[44] Is this yearning man's great misfortune? Ought the humanization of man to be the healing of his wish for God? What would happen if man were to lose the taste for this yearning? The Christian tradition has always attributed to man a *desiderium naturale* for the deifying vision of God, but it has equally insisted that this yearning can attain its goal only thanks to an *exaltation* of man by God, when he is given resemblance and relatedness to God.[45] It is only through such an exaltation that man realizes his deepest aspirations. For the Christian tradition, there is no genuine "humanization" of man without an "exaltation above himself". Paradoxically, it does not suffice to be a mere man in order to be a true man. If he does not seek his perfecting in God

[43] Cf. C. S. Lewis, *The Abolition of Man* (Oxford, 1943).

[44] Paris, 1943, 653f.

[45] Numerous texts in H. de Lubac, *Le Mystère du Surnaturel* (Paris, 1965), 105–33.

(Thomas says, *Deus enim solus satiat*, "God alone satisfies"),[46] then his yearning, which cannot be extirpated, turns to the things of this world in order to find its appeasing there. The search for bliss becomes the search for enjoyment; the source of true happiness is replaced by a world full of deified things. But man's heart is not satisfied by any substitute.

But when "things" take the place of God, then man demands of them something that they cannot give. By seeking in them this something "more", he perverts his relationship to things; he wants to wrest from the world a joy that only the bliss of God can bestow on him gratis. The world no longer appears to him as the work of God, which he is allowed to use with reverence and thanks: he sees it only from the perspective of what profit it brings him, since he is incapable of seeing it as what it is in itself. Deifying the world, all that he can do now is to ravish it and exploit it for himself, and this exploitation could lead today to its destruction. The deification of the world is the ultimate expression of man's self-deification.[47]

According to some contemporary thinkers, the "megalomania of the yearning" for deification is the

[46] *In Symbol. Apost.* 12.

[47] Maximus the Confessor gave a very acute analysis of this connection, which is still relevant today; cf. my essay on "Lust und Schmerz in der Analyse des heiligen Maximus nach den *Quaestiones ad Thalassium*", in *Maximus Confessor, Actes du Symposium sur Maxime le Confesseur, Fribourg, 2.–5. Sept. 1980*, ed. F. Heinzer and C. Schönborn (Fribourg, 1982), 273–84.

cause of the threats that weigh down upon our world: the destruction of the world and the self-destruction of man.[48] The solution, however, lies not (as is asserted) in extinguishing this yearning but in its correct orientation. It is not the greatness of the yearning but its perversion that threatens man. If this yearning is kept closed in on itself, it can only destroy man. If it is opened out onto its true goal, it can lead to receiving God's bliss, which is the only valid answer to human yearning. It "more than realizes" (so to speak) all man's expectation.[49]

Grace exalts us and makes us like God. It gives us the capacity to receive infinite happiness and divine bliss, for which God created us,[50] and for which we do not cease to strive, even through the error of self-deification.

[48] Cf. H. E. Richter, *Der Gotteskomplex. Die Geburt und die Krise des Glaubens an die Allmacht des Menschen* (Hamburg, 1979).

[49] Cf. Anastasius Sinaiticus, *Hodêgos* II, 7, 8–9 (ed. Uthemann); PG 89, 77 B: "Deification is the exaltation to that which is better; it is no reduction or alteration of the nature."

[50] Thomas says that through grace *ipsa natura hominis elevatur ad quamdam dignitatem, secundum quam talis finis sit ei competens* (*De ver.* q. 27, a. 2).

Chapter III

THE KINGDOM OF GOD
AND THE HEAVENLY-EARTHLY CHURCH:
THE CHURCH IN TRANSITION
ACCORDING TO *LUMEN GENTIUM*

"God, who is rich in mercy, out of the great love with which he loved us, has made even us, who were dead through our sins, alive together with Christ . . . and he has raised us up with him in Christ Jesus and given us a place with him in the heavens" (Eph 2:4–6). Christian existence means being with Christ, and thus means being where he is, "sitting at the right hand of the Father" (cf. Chapter 1). The Church has her homeland where Christ is. In terms of her Head and of her goal, she is a *heavenly* Church. Since she is an earthly Church, she knows that she is a *pilgrim* Church, stretching out to reach her goal.

The Second Vatican Council's Constitution on the Church, *Lumen gentium* (= LG), contemplated the

This text was read to the plenary assembly of the International Theological Commission in October 1984. Cf. also now the document of the International Theological Commission, *Mysterium des Gottesvolkes* (Einsiedeln, 1987), which was drawn up at this plenary assembly.

Church as the people of God. If one reads this great conciliar text as a whole, it is clear that the Council sees the Church as the people of God entirely on the basis of her *goal*, to be the heavenly, perfected Church (cf. LG 2). It is only the goal that gives meaning to the path. The Church is the pilgrim people of God, and her goal is the heavenly Jerusalem. It is only when we contemplate the Church in her earthly-heavenly transitional existence that we have the *whole* Church in view. This is why we begin (1) by presenting some witnesses for this way of seeing the Church; then we ask (2) why the sensitivity to this perspective has been largely lost today, and above all why the heavenly dimension of the Church is often forgotten; finally (3), we should like to indicate some perspectives on how it is possible to regain this vision of the Church as heavenly-earthly reality. The seventh chapter of *Lumen gentium* will give us special help in understanding here.

1. One Single Church of Heaven and of Earth

a. *The Unity of the Pilgrim Church and the Heavenly Church*

Andrea Pozzo has given a most beautiful expression, in a painting on the ceiling of Sant'Ignazio in Rome, to the unity of the pilgrim Church and the Church of heaven. On the ceiling of the central nave, a great Baroque architecture opens out onto an infinite heaven.

Saint Ignatius ascends on clouds to the Holy Trinity. Other saints of the Society of Jesus join him; on all sides, angels ascend and descend, creating the link here to the allegorical representations of the four continents, which strive toward this heavenly fellowship and make their way toward it. While the Church of heaven descends, the pilgrim Church ascends to her native land; or rather, both make their way to meet one another, "grow together to form the one Church" to which all her members belong "to various extents and in various ways" (LG 49), whether they are pilgrims on earth or "have departed from this life and are being purified" or are already glorified in the vision of God (LG 49).

In the church of Sant'Ignazio there is also the tomb of Saint Robert Bellarmine, who dedicated an entire volume of his work *De controversiis christianae fidei* to the three levels of the Church: the Church militant, the Church of the state of purification, and the triumphant Church.[1] The ecclesiology of the Counter-Reformation has often been accused of overemphasizing the societal, institutional character of the Church militant and giving

[1] When the much-discussed definition of the Church by Saint Robert Bellarmine ("The Church is an association of men which is just as visible and tangible as the association of the Roman people or of the kingdom of France or of the republic of Venice", in vol. II, *Contr.* 1ª, Liber III, cap. II) is criticized today, it is all too easily forgotten that it concerns only the aspect of the Church militant and that it must be given its place within the totality of the three levels of the Church. Cf. the observations by Charles Journet, *L'Eglise du Verbe Incarné*, vol. II, 61 in a footnote and 80.

too little prominence to her fundamentally eschatological character. By replacing the expression "Church militant" with the concept of "pilgrim Church",[2] the
Council wanted to correct this vision and to show that
the Church in her pilgrim state strives with all her might
toward her fullness and perfection "in the heavenly
glory" (LG 48). Chapter VII of *Lumen gentium* was ed-
ited in this perspective, even if "belatedly and hur-
riedly".[3] John XXIII and Paul VI had personally insisted
with vigor on the introduction of some remarks on the
veneration of the saints at some place in the Constitution on the Church. The Council took the view that
the question of the veneration of the saints must be situ-
ated against a wider theological horizon, namely, that of
the eschatological character of the Church. Monsignor
Gerard Philips makes the following comments on the
outcome of this work:

> This idea leads us unexpectedly to a happy enrichment of
> the Constitution on the Church. Not only does this broad-
> ening permit us to see the Church in her totality, including
> her perfection: it also proffers us the meaning of her

[2] The expression "militant" Church crops up again, a little surpris-
ingly, in L. Boff, *Iglesia: carisma y poder. Ensayos de ecclesiología militante*
(1982).

[3] H. de Lubac, *Geheimnis aus dem wir leben* (Einsiedeln, 1967), 105. Cf.
the commentaries by Msgr. G. Philips, *L'Eglise et son mystère*, vol. II (Paris,
1968), 161–205, and O. Semmelroth in *Lexikon für Theologie und Kirche*,
Supplement I, Das Zweite Vatikanische Konzil, 314–25. It is striking that
chap. 7 has found little echo in what has been written about LG. Cf., however, C. Pozzo, *Teología del Más Allá*, 2nd ed. (Madrid, 1980), 538–78.

marching forward, in concrete terms the meaning of hope. Only now are we able to understand completely Chapter II, on the pilgrim people of God. The second and the penultimate [seventh] chapters of *Lumen gentium* correspond to one another and achieve the equilibrium. Now we no longer merely consider whence we come and what has already been realized: we consider also the direction in which we are heading and what awaits us in the future.[4]

Although this vision does a little to correct the insufficiently eschatological view of the "Church militant" in the posttridentine theology, "it remains true that the decision to take 'people of God' as the fundamental and initial concept, linked with today's juxtaposition of the two Churches—the earthly, in which we live, and the heavenly Church of those who have already reached their 'native land'—has brought about a certain restriction of the patristic horizon."[5]

One must indeed take care not to exaggerate this antithesis and push it to extremes.[6] Nevertheless, it is useful to point it out.

b. *The Church Is Essentially Heavenly*

Cardinal Henri de Lubac emphasizes a certain difference between the patristic view and the view presented by *Lumen gentium*. What is this difference?

[4] Msgr. G. Philips, *L'Eglise*, 163f.
[5] H. de Lubac, *Geheimnis*, 110f.
[6] Ibid., 107.

"You have come", says the Letter to the Hebrews, "to
Mount Zion, to the city of the living God, to the Jerusalem above." Our fathers believed these words and
reflected on them. Thus, the Church that had given birth
to them in the water of baptism—precisely this earthly,
visible Church—was at the same time "the heavenly
Church" for them, "the new Jerusalem above, our
mother". "Let us already now, in the Church, live in the
Jerusalem above", Augustine will say, "so that we may
not perish for ever" (*In psalm.* 124, no. 4). And again:
"The present Church is the kingdom of Christ and the
kingdom of God" (*Sermo* 125). In this synthesizing vision
of the mystery, the Church is identified with Christ her
Bridegroom, who is himself the kingdom: *autobasileia*, in
Origen's wonderful term. And precisely this vision corresponds to the deepest logic of Christian eschatology: if
one were to abandon it, countless abuses in thought and
deed would be the result.[7]

In my view, some of the directions taken by ecclesiology that have emerged since the Council justify the
anxiety that Cardinal de Lubac had formulated already
before the Council. I shall attempt to show that one
cannot understand such tendencies to be the view of
the Council itself. Before we tackle these disputed questions, let us first remain with this vision of the Church
as a reality that is essentially heavenly. The following
testimonies—basically chance fruits of my reading—do
not claim to offer a fully rounded picture, but feature

[7] Ibid., 111.

here as harmonious voices (so to speak) in the immeasurable choir of the Church.

The Church is where Christ is. How then would it be possible for her not to be primarily in heaven, where Christ is? A nun who lived in secret in Hungary and died at the age of twenty-five writes in her diary:

> This Easter feast was the first that permitted me to experience what I have accepted with my understanding for a very long time: this life is only a brief passage of transition that flies quickly away. The only truth is the risen Lord. It is still painful to be far away from him, and how much do I feel this on this day! But I can never again forget this unique experience, which lasted only a few minutes. It is not this life that is reality for me: the other life, beyond the grave, is a thousand times more real.[8]

It is impossible not to be reminded of Paul here. "You have been raised up with Christ: therefore strive for the things that are in heaven, where Christ sits at the right hand of God" (Col 3:1; cf. LG 6 and 48); "Thus we are always confident, even though we know that we live in exile far from the Lord, as long as we are at home in this body; for we walk as those who believe, not as those who see. But because we are confident, we prefer to depart from the body and to be at home with the Lord" (2 Cor 5:6–8; cf. LG 6, 48, 49); "I yearn to depart and to be with Christ" (Phil 1:23; cf. LG 48).

---

[8] *Monika. Ein Zeugnis in Ungarn*, with introduction by H. U. von Balthasar (Einsiedeln, 1982), 160.

This experience, this faith, this burning desire do not come from a pagan egotism that aims at one's own immortality (that was the objection of an Adolph von Harnack).[9] Their center is Christ himself and his promise: "There are many dwellings in my Father's house. . . . I go to prepare a place for you. When I have gone and have prepared a place for you, I will come again and take you to myself, so that you too may be where I am" (Jn 14:2–3). The Jerusalem Bible comments on this text: "The entire expectation of the Church is based on this promise." For here is the place of her hope. Thanks to Christ, the faithful have already here below their "native land in heaven" (Phil 3:20; cf. LG 48); they are "no longer foreigners without the rights of citizens, but fellow-citizens of the saints and members of God's household" (Eph 2:19; cf. LG 6); their names have been entered in the list of the citizens of the heavenly Jerusalem (cf. Lk 10:20). "All the faithful who are pilgrims on this earth make for the 'city of the living God' and do not cease to go toward it (Heb 12:22)."[10] "The heavenly Jerusalem . . . is our mother" (Gal 4:26; cf. LG 6). Thus, to be a Christian means that one has set up his tent in heaven

---

[9] *Das Wesen des Christentums*, Akad. Ausg. Leipzig, 146.

[10] C. Spicq, "Les chrétiens vivent en citoyens du ciel", in idem, *Théologie morale du Nouveau Testament*, vol. 1 (Paris, 1970), 417–32, at 418; cf. by the same author, *Vie chrétienne et pérégrination selon le Nouveau Testament* (Paris, 1972); cf. also E. Peterson, "Von den Engeln", in idem, *Theologische Traktate* (Munich, 1951), 327–29.

(Rev 12:12 and 13:6).[11] Because Christ is her Head, and she his Body, the Church is essentially heavenly. Augustine says this again and again: " 'Jerusalem, which is constructed as a city': Christ is its foundation. The Apostle Paul says: 'No one can lay any other foundation than that which is already laid: Jesus Christ' (1 Cor 3:11). When the foundation is laid in the earth, the walls are built above it, and the weight of the walls pulls downward, because the foundation is laid below. But if our foundation is in heaven, we will be built up toward heaven . . . , for . . . we are constructed in a spiritual manner; our foundation lies above. Let us then hasten to the place where we are being built!" [12]

This mighty vision of the Church is not in the least an evasion that would permit one to avoid the toils and vicissitudes of an active involvement in this world. It is only when one sees in faith the "heavenly" nature of the Church that the meaning of her earthly condition as a pilgrim Church becomes clear as well. Since she has her origin in the life of God himself, in the Holy Trinity, the Church is "first of all a reality founded by heaven in time".[13] She is this because she is nothing other than what God intends to do with this world, according to the

[11] According to E.-B. Allo, *L'Apocalypse* (Paris, 1933), 208, these passages (cf. also Rev 7:15) concern also "the dwelling of God in the hearts of the saints, already here below through grace, and then in heaven".

[12] *Enarr. in Ps.* CXXI, 4; PL 37, 1621; cf. the numerous texts in H. de Lubac, *Die Kirche. Eine Betrachtung* (Einsiedeln, 1968), 66–71.

[13] H. U. von Balthasar, *Theodramatik. Das Endspiel* (= vol. IV) (Einsiedeln, 1983), 114; cf. the texts of Adrienne von Speyr quoted ibid., 114–

famous saying of Clement of Alexandria: "For as his will
is a deed, and this deed is called 'world', so is also his desire the salvation of men, and this is called 'Church'." [14]
In this ultimate vision there lies the final meaning of the
"communion of saints" that we profess in the creed. Ni-
cetas of Remesiana has expressed this vividly:

> After you have professed your faith in the most blessed
> Trinity, you declare that you believe in the holy Catholic
> Church. What is the Church other than the gathering to-
> gether of all the saints? For since the beginning of the
> world, the patriarchs . . . , the prophets, the martyrs, and
> all the righteous . . . form one single Church, since they
> are sanctified through one and the same faith and one and
> the same life, and are marked with the sign of one and the
> same Spirit, and thus form one single Body. As is stated
> above, Christ is termed the Head of this Body. But there
> is still more to be said. Even the angels, the heavenly dom-
> inations, and authorities are members of this one single
> Church. . . . Believe therefore that you are to attain to the
> fellowship of the saints in this one Church. Know that this
> Catholic Church is *one*, established over the whole face of
> the earth; you must cling decisively to her fellowship. [15]

22: The Church is "in a very proper sense the place where eternity begins within time"; "The Church with all her sacraments and institutions
lives from the air of eternity of heaven; she cannot avoid mediating
something of this." Cf. also H. U. von Balthasar, "Die himmlische
Kirche und ihre Erscheinung", in idem, *Homo creatus est* (Einsiedeln,
1986), 148–64 (= *Skizzen zur Theologie*, vol. v).

[14] *Paedagogus* I, chap. VI, 27, 2.

[15] *Explanatio Symboli*, 10: PL 52, 871 B; cf. P.-Y. Emery, "L'unité des
croyants au ciel et sur la terre", in *Verbum Caro* 16 (1962), no. 63, 1–240.

We asked whether in Andrea Pozzo's ceiling painting it is the Church of heaven that is descending or the Church of earth that is ascending. Now we can say: it is the one single Church of heaven and of earth. But since this one single Church has her true dwelling place in heaven, she is in her essence "the holy city, the new Jerusalem that comes down from God out of heaven" (Rev 21:2). In the course of the centuries, Christian art and architecture have endeavored to express this, by making churches into images of the heavenly Jerusalem.

2. Disputed Questions

a. *The Church and the Kingdom of God*

"Who is the city of God, if not the holy Church? " [16] Is the Church identical with the kingdom of God? Augustine affirms this: "Thus, the Church is already now the kingdom of Christ and the kingdom of heaven";[17] although it is true that the kingdom of Christ here below (*nunc*) is "in a state of war (*militae*)"; it will be perfected only at the end of the ages (*in fine saeculorum, tunc*).[18]

---

[16] Augustine, *En. in Ps.* XCII, no. 4; cf. *De civ. Dei* XVI, 2, 3; cf. n. 28, pp. 774–77 ("L'Eglise et la Cité de Dieu") in vol. 37 of the *Oeuvres de Saint Augustin* (Paris, 1960).

[17] *De civ. Dei* XX, 9, 1.

[18] Ibid., 1 and 2; cf. the note on "les deux états de l'Eglise 'qualis nunc' et 'qualis tunc' ", in the *Oeuvres de Saint Augustin*, vol. 32 (Paris, 1965), 723–25.

Thomas Aquinas does not say anything different: "The kingdom of God is spoken of by preference (as it were) in a double sense: first, as the group of those who walk in faith, and in this sense the Church militant is called the 'kingdom of God'; but then also as the assembly of those who have already safely attained their goal, and in this sense the triumphant Church is called the 'kingdom of God'." [19]

For both Augustine and Thomas, there are two successive states of the Church, *nunc et tunc*, now and then: the definitive and the provisional state of the kingdom of God. Jacques Bonsirven says the same in his book *Le Règne de Dieu*: "Is the kingdom of God identical with the Church. . . ? The answer can only be 'yes'." [20] Cardinal Charles Journet is no less affirmative: "We do not believe that one can refuse to identify the Church and the kingdom. We have two concepts here, but only one single reality. The Church is the kingdom; the kingdom is the Church. The concept of 'kingdom' refers to eschatology. But it is precisely with Jesus that eschatology, which belongs above all to the qualitative order, has broken into time. From the time of Christ onward, the whole Church has entered the end time; she is eschatological." [21]

But now, precisely in the name of eschatology, this

---

[19] *In IV Sent.*, d. 49, q. 1, a. 2, quaest. 5, sol. 5.

[20] Paris, 1957, 194f.

[21] *L'Eglise du Verbe Incarné*, vol. II (Bruges, 1951), 997, n. 1; cf. 60–91 and *Nova et Vetera* 38 (1963), 307–10.

identification has been called into question for about
the last one hundred years in a debate that is not at all
concluded. Much is at stake here, for it is a question not
only of the nature of the Church but also of very
significant practical consequences. If the Church is essentially heavenly, since she is "there where Christ is",
if she is his Body, and it is "not only the believers who
are alive today that belong" to this Body "but also those
who have lived before us, and those who will come
after us until the end of time",[22] then it is not possible
to grasp a reason *not* to identify the Church and the
kingdom of God. The objection has been made for a
hundred years that one may not identify the Church
with the kingdom, since this is a strictly eschatological
reality, whereas the Church is only a sign of the kingdom and a pointer to it. We must attempt to clarify this
very confused question, so we shall begin by listening
carefully to the teaching of the Council, and then we
shall ask about the reception of this teaching.

b. *Is the "Eschatological Character of the Pilgrim
   Church" (LG 48) the Eschatological Character
   of the Kingdom of God?*

One can often read the statement that the Council
taught that the Church is *the sacrament of the kingdom*:
"The Council has given new vigor to the old patristic

---

[22] Augustine, *En. in Ps.* LXII, no. 2.

view of the Church as the sacrament of the kingdom.
. . . In her [the pilgrim Church], the kingdom of God is
already present. She is, as Augustine says, already 'the
reconciled world', she is already the new creation; but
she is this 'according to the mystery', 'sacramentally';
she is not yet the kingdom in its fullness and its
definitive realization." [23] But if the author of these lines
had looked more closely, he could have seen that the
council nowhere calls the Church the "sacrament of the
kingdom".

The Constitution *Lumen gentium* is clear on this
point. It states in no. 3: "In order to accomplish the Father's will, Christ founded the kingdom of heaven on
earth, revealed his mystery to us, and brought about our
redemption through his obedience. The Church, i.e.,
the kingdom of Christ which is already present in mystery, grows visibly in the world through the power of
God." Before we ask what "already present in mystery"
may mean here, let us listen to two other texts of the
Constitution.

Article 5, which was inserted in the schema after the
discussions of the second conciliar session, is entirely
concerned with the Church and the kingdom of God.
The *Relatio commissionis doctrinalis* states that this article,

---

[23] I myself "perpetrated" these sentences in *Realizzare il Concilio. Il con-
tributo di Communione e Liberazione* (Milan, 1982), in a lecture on "Il
significato ecclesiologico del Concilio Ecumenico Vaticano II", at 23. This
text, which I hereby withdraw, was also published in the *Osservatore Ro-
mano* on October 2, 1982, under the title "Realizzare il Concilio" (p. 2).

which originally bore the title "On the kingdom of God", was inserted because it expressed the simultaneously visible and spiritual character of the Church's fellowship, as well as her historical and eschatological aspect.[24] Although one really should quote the whole text, which is very important for our subject, we limit ourselves to recalling the following striking passages: "For the Lord Jesus initiated his Church by proclaiming the good news, namely the coming of the kingdom of God, which had been promised from of old in the Scriptures: 'The time is fulfilled, and the kingdom of God has drawn near' (Mk 1:15; cf. Mt 4:17)." The presence of the kingdom is seen in the words and works, but above all in the person, of Christ himself. Christ's mission is continued in the Church: "The Church receives thence . . . the mission to proclaim the kingdom of God and of Christ and to establish it among all peoples. Thus she represents the seed and the beginning of this kingdom. As she gradually grows, she reaches out in longing for the perfected kingdom; with all her might she hopes and yearns to be united with her King in glory."

The Church is here called the "seed and beginning of this kingdom" on earth. May one comment on this as follows: "This is why the Church can posit a distance between the Church and Christ: she is only the sacrament of salvation. It can proclaim the distance between

[24] Quoted from G. Alberigo and F. Magistretti (eds.), *Constitutionis Dogmaticae Lumen Gentium Synopsis Historica* (Bologna, 1975), 436.

the Church and the kingdom: here too we have an 'already and not yet' (cf. LG 5, above all the conclusion; UR 2, 5). Because the Church is not coterminous with the kingdom, she renews and reforms herself unceasingly: LG 8, 3 conclusion; GS 21, 5: 43, 6". [25]

Is the purpose of the formulations, "present in mystery" (LG 3) and "seed and beginning" (LG 5), "to proclaim the distance between the Church and the kingdom"? A third text can complete the framework of this question. LG 9 says of the people of God: "This messianic people has Christ as its Head. . . . It is destined to possess the kingdom of God, which was founded on earth by God himself and must continue to unfold until it is also perfected by him at the end of the ages." Is this text to be read in the sense of a distance between the Church and the kingdom? In my view, the answer can be given only on the basis of the Constitution *Lumen gentium* as a whole: for if we read these three passages in the light of Chapter VII, it becomes clear that one can speak of a "distance" only when one

[25] Thus Y. Congar, "Les implications christologiques et pneumatologiques de l'Ecclésiologie de Vatican II", in idem, *Le Concile de Vatican II. Son Eglise, peuple de Dieu et corps du Christ* (Paris, 1984), 174 (= Théologie historique 71). With the exception of the first (LG 5), none of the passages adduced here speaks of the kingdom of God: UR 3, 5 states that the Church is on the pilgrimage of hope toward "the fullness of eternal glory in the heavenly Jerusalem"; LG 8, 3 says that the Church is "at once holy and always in need of purification"; LG 9 (conclusion) adds that she is "ceaselessly renewing herself"; GS 21, 5 takes over LG 8, 3; GS 43, 6 takes over LG 15, where the members of the Church are summoned to purification.

is looking at the Church in her *pilgrim existence*. Seen in this way, she is not yet the *perfected* kingdom: "In her sacraments and institutions, which still belong to this period of the world, the pilgrim Church bears the figure of this world which is passing away" (LG 48). Does this mean that she stands at a distance from the kingdom?

The pilgrim Church is nothing other than the "kingdom of heaven" that Christ has established on earth (LG 3). When it is said of the pilgrim Church that she is "the kingdom of Christ which is already present in mystery" (ibid.) and that she is the "seed and beginning of this kingdom on earth" (LG 5), then the perfected kingdom will be nothing other than the perfected Church: "It is only in heavenly glory . . . that the Church will be perfected" (LG 48). Will this Church, when she is "perfected in glory at the end of the ages of the world" (LG 2), be anything other than the totally realized kingdom? For "then will . . . all the righteous . . . be gathered together in the Father's presence in the all-embracing Church" (ibid.). It is certainly true that the Church strives with all her power "to attain the perfected kingdom" (LG 5), but in this "she yearns to be united with her King in glory" (ibid.), and as long as she goes along the paths of her earthly pilgrimage, her life is nevertheless "hidden with Christ in God, until she appears in glory, united to her Bridegroom (cf. Col 3:1–4)" (LG 6).

Thus there lies no distance between the Church and

the kingdom of God. Rather, we have different *status*
both of the Church and of the kingdom: The *pilgrim*
Church is the kingdom that "buds and grows until the
time for the harvest (cf. Mk 4:26–29) " (LG 5), but the
Church in the glory of heaven is the perfected kingdom, the final goal of the pilgrimage of the messianic
people of God (cf. LG 9).

But what then shall we say about the fact that the
Church, which "includes sinners within her own self, is
at one and the same time holy and continuously in need
of purification, and always takes the path of penitence
and renewal" (LG 8)? Is this "because the Church is not
coterminous with the kingdom" ? As we have seen (cf.
note 25), the Council never makes such a connection.
On the contrary, the Council clearly demonstrates, by
appealing to the Gospel, that the kingdom that Christ
initiated on earth has no other destiny than the Church:
"The word of the Lord is like a seed that is sown in a
field (cf. Mk 4:14): those who hear it in faith and are
counted among the little flock of Christ (cf. Lk 12:32)
have received the kingdom itself" (LG 5). The saints
make known how the Church is already the kingdom
received in faith. "In their life . . . God shows men in a
living manner his presence and his countenance. In
them, he himself speaks to us and gives us a sign of his
kingdom, to which we are powerfully drawn, sur-
rounded as we are by such a great cloud of witnesses
(cf. Heb 12:1) and confronted with such a testimony to
the truth of the Gospel" (LG 50).

The Church *is* the kingdom, and the Council does not permit us to say that she is merely its sacrament. For the expression *sacrament* is in fact employed by the Council in another sense, which strengthens even further the identity between the Church and the kingdom: "Christ has . . . made his Body, the Church, the all-embracing sacrament of salvation" (LG 48). "For the Church is in Christ as it were the sacrament, i.e., the sign and the instrument, for the most intimate uniting to God, the unity of the whole of humanity" (LG 1). The sacramentality of the Church lies in her relationship to the world—not to the kingdom. Through her and in her, Christ calls all men to himself: "Sitting at the right hand of the Father, he works continuously in the world to lead men to the Church and to unite them more closely to himself through her" (LG 48). Paul VI summarized the teaching of the Council in his "Credo of the People of God": "We profess that the kingdom of God begins here on earth in the Church of Christ" (no. 35). Cardinal Journet says the same in a summarizing formulation: "The kingdom is already on earth, and the Church is already in heaven. To abandon the equal value of Church and kingdom would mean overlooking this important revelation." [26]

---

[26] *L'Eglise du Verbe Incarné*, vol. II, 57.

c. *"The Fata Morgana of Eschatology"* [27]

On January 28, 1979, Pope John Paul II addressed the following words to the Latin American bishops at Puebla:

> In the extensive material drawn up in preparation for this conference . . . one sometimes notices a certain confusion in the exposition of the nature and mission of the Church. For example, we find the reference to the separation that some make between the Church and the kingdom of God. This deprives the kingdom of its full contents, so that it is understood in a very secularized sense: thus we are told that one does not enter the kingdom of God through faith and through belonging to the Church.[28]

To what confusion does the Holy Father refer here? Which secularization of the concept "kingdom of God" is involved here? The problem to which he alludes is basically an old problem, but one that has taken on a new form in roughly the last hundred years. The secularization of the idea of the kingdom of God is one of the possible consequences of the radical eschatologism that has dominated the discussions about the relationship between the Church and the kingdom of God since Johannes Weiss, Alfred Loisy, and Albert Schweit-

---

[27] *Le mirage de l'Eschatologie* is the title of what I consider a very important book by the recently deceased French exegete Jean Carmignac (Paris, 1979). This well-documented book has the subtitle "Royauté, Règne et Royaume de Dieu . . . sans Eschatologie".

[28] AAS 71, no. 3 (February 1979), 194.

zer. We cannot sketch here the history of this debate, which is not yet in the least closed. We limit ourselves to the presentation by J. Carmignac (see note 27) and to the theses that Leonardo Boff has developed in his "Ecclesiogenesis".[29]

Jean Carmignac begins by recalling that the source of many obscurities about the kingdom of God is the fact that Greek has only one expression, *basileia*, to reproduce three Hebrew expressions that are close to but not identical with it: *melukah* (kingdom), *malkuth* (lordship), and *mamlakah* (the land ruled by a king).[30] Naturally, the interpretation of the scriptural texts acquires greater precision when one takes into account the particular aspect involved in each individual use of the expression *basileia*.[31] Then it becomes clear that, whereas one can distinguish the Church in some way from the lordship of God, one cannot distinguish her from the "sphere where the King rules". "*De facto*, the various traits of this kingdom of God or of Christ correspond to those of the Church." [32] Carmignac summarizes the results of his exegetical investigation as follows:

> It is not permissible . . . as some writers do, to see the Church as a preparation for the kingdom, for then the

[29] *Eclesiogênese. As comunidades de base reinventam a Igreja* (Petrópolis, 1977), quoted here from the German edition, *Die Neuentdeckung der Kirche. Basisgemeinden in Lateinamerika* (Mainz, 1980).

[30] Ibid., 13–16.

[31] Ibid., 19–83.

[32] Ibid., 99.

kingdom would be temporally later than the Church, and that would contradict the words of Jesus and the apostles, who confirm that the kingdom already belongs to their time and is a present reality. Nor may one hold the view that the kingdom of God will be the continuation of the Church in the other world. The Church began to exist at precisely the moment in which the kingdom of God was founded, and she will continue to exist for the whole of eternity. It is not at all possible to separate the Church and the kingdom from one another—at least, not if one holds to the New Testament as a whole, without giving some texts preference before others.

But the identification of the Church and the kingdom of God does not in the least oblige us to see these two expressions as synonymous. They refer to the same reality, but from different perspectives. If one speaks of the kingdom of God, one looks above all at the event of God's working, which is realized among men when they gather around Christ; if one speaks of the Church, one looks above all at these men who are gathered around Christ by God.[33]

Carmignac draws up an impressive list of authors from the Church Fathers on into our own days who make statements in keeping with this identification.[34] Why therefore has this identity lost its evidential character from a certain point in time that does not lie very far in the past? Here begins what Carmignac calls "the fata morgana of eschatology". The "formation of an

[33] Ibid., 101.
[34] Ibid., 102–19.

error" begins with Reimarus; it consists in the idea, which has been vigorously propagated since then, that the entire Jewish people at the time of Jesus awaited the kingdom of the Messiah. Eduard Reuss extends this idea by means of the assertion that Jesus' contemporaries lived in an eschatological "high tension". Ernest Renan popularizes the idea that Jesus too lived in this "high tension" and that he awaited the imminent, abrupt irruption of the kingdom of God as the total overthrowing of this world.

"Basically, the considerations of these authors went astray because of two fundamental errors: (a) because of rationalistic prejudices, they bracketed off (consciously or not) those texts of the New Testament that opposed their theory and did not agree with their prefabricated syntheses; (b) they imagined that the Jews at the beginning of the Christian era were obsessed by the expectation of the kingdom of God and that Jesus shared their illusions." [35] The "success of an error" was ensured by Johannes Weiss and Alfred Loisy. Both men "take one further step, because they begin to combine the concepts 'kingdom of God' (as something lying exclusively in the future) and 'eschatology' (reified to become the end of the world). For them, eschatology and the kingdom of God become two correlative concepts that cannot be separated from one another." [36] Two theses take on an uncritically accepted evidential character for

[35] Ibid., 144f.
[36] Ibid., 147.

many: "that Jesus' contemporaries lived *in the feverish expectation of the kingdom of God* and that *Jesus* could do no other than make *their illusions* his own".[37] The "triumph of an error" arrives with Albert Schweitzer. "Schweitzer presupposes without further ado that the *kingdom of God* is a *purely eschatological* vision of faith, and he constructs inexorably a life of Jesus that goes in circles around this illusion, which was to be proved to be a lie by the historical reality." [38] The "logic of an error" reaches its zenith in Rudolph Bultmann. For him, it is clear "that *Jesus' proclamation of God's lordship* was an eschatological message" and that this was "the message of the coming end of the world". "All this means that in earliest Christianity *history was swallowed up by eschatology*." [39]

W. G. Kümmel observes on this point: "This fundamentally futurist-eschatological understanding of Jesus' proclamation, with its basis laid by Johannes Weiss and Albert Schweitzer, seems to be for Bultmann so much a matter of course that he neither adduces any evidence in support of it nor mentions any dissenting opinions." [40]

The most striking thing about the dossier drawn up by Carmignac is the demonstration that there exists no

[37] Ibid., 154.

[38] Ibid., 157.

[39] *Geschichte und Eschatologie* (Tübingen, 1958), 36–42.

[40] "Die Naherwartung in der Verkündigung Jesu", in *Zeit und Geschichte* (Festschrift for Bultmann) (Tübingen, 1964), 31–46, at 31.

evidence for this view of eschatology and of the kingdom of God. The few texts that are usually plucked out
of the intertestamental literature and adduced as evidence do not in the least permit one to construct the
entire theory of eschatologism upon them.[41] Thus the
presumed apocalyptic horizon that Jesus allegedly shared
with his contemporaries shrinks greatly, and one must
ask whether eschatologism is not to a great extent an *a
priori* construction. Before we return to this question,
we shall look briefly at the consequences to which the
"fata morgana of eschatology" can lead.

In his "Ecclesiogenesis" (cf. note 29), *Leonardo Boff*
takes over the theses of eschatologism and makes them
his own without posing any questions—simply as a
matter of course. The explosive quality of his views
comes from the practical consequences that he draws
from this position. Boff takes it for granted that Jesus
lived in the imminent eschatological expectation of the
kingdom of God:[42] "No one can deny that Jesus had
the same temporal expectation as his entire generation." [43]

The necessary inference from the supposition that
people at that period were expecting the kingdom of
God, understood as the end of the world, and that it
was precisely *this* kingdom of God that Jesus pro-

[41] Cf. J. Carmignac, *Le mirage*, 160–65; cf. 212f.

[42] L. Boff, *Eclesiogênese*, first *quaestio disputata*, 3.4 (p. 80 of German
ed.).

[43] Ibid., 90. One is surprised at the assuredness of this assertion.

claimed, is that Jesus did not wish to found the Church, but rather to proclaim this kingdom. Jesus' "imminent expectation" seems of itself to exclude the idea that he thought of an institutionally established Church.[44] For Boff, it is a fact that Jesus' expectation was not fulfilled. The kingdom did not come—at least, it did not come in the form in which it was expected. Thanks to the death and then the Resurrection of Jesus, the kingdom of God became reality in the person of Jesus. But the kingdom has not become universally realized; it has found its personal realization in Jesus, and this realization is the anticipation of the fullness of the kingdom. And it is here that the Church finds her place and her possibility of existence: "Thus the Church has clearly the character of a substitute for the kingdom of God. On the one hand, she is the kingdom of God, since the Risen One lives in her; on the other hand, she is also not the kingdom, since it is only in the end time that the kingdom of God will come. The Church is at the service of the kingdom of God and is its sacrament, sign, and instrument, so that it can start and realize itself in the world." [45]

The Church—as the link that spans the gap between Easter and the delayed parousia—is thus the "substitute" for the kingdom, which is understood as a purely eschatological reality. One is, accordingly, not surprised when it is stated that the Church owes her existence

[44] Ibid., 82–84 (= nos. 8–12).
[45] Ibid., 91.

not to any intention of the "pre-Easter Jesus" but to a decision taken by Peter and the apostles, namely, the decision to begin the mission to the Gentiles:[46] "As an institution, therefore, the Church is based not (as is generally asserted) on the Incarnation of the Word but on the faith and the power of the apostles, who transposed eschatology into the time of the Church, thanks to the might of the Spirit, and translated the message about the kingdom of God into the teaching about the Church—the Church, which is an imperfect and temporal realization of the kingdom." [47]

Here we see to the full the serious consequences of "the fata morgana of eschatology": a narrowed-down understanding of the kingdom (bereft of its present element as something that is "already there") is linked to a reductionist understanding of the Church (which is bereft of her "eschatological character"). This has grave consequences, for such a Church—detached from the plan of Jesus Christ and bound one-sidedly to the working of the spirit [48]—is based on human, and thus mutable, decisions. Thus the ecclesiogenesis, the "new birth of the Church", which the author foresees can be brought about through new decisions: "The Church can organize herself in a manner different to that hitherto prevailing, because this is theologically possible

[46] Ibid., 87.

[47] Ibid., 95f.

[48] Cf. the criticism of this position in Congar, "Les implications", 165f.

and because this lies in the intention of Jesus Christ." [49] What institutional form is the Church to have? "Jesus wanted, and still wants, the form for which the apostolic fellowship decides, out of the power of the Spirit and in confrontation with the needs of each individual situation, and which this fellowship makes its own." [50]

Yves Congar observes, "This certainly does not correspond to the intention of the Council." [51] In my view, the fundamental defect in this view of the Church lies in its Christology. This ecclesiology is the product of a reductionist Christology.[52] If the Council's vision of the Church is to be received more fully and deeply, the christological bases of *Lumen gentium* must be considered anew.

3. Theological and Pastoral Tasks in View of a More Complete Reception of *Lumen Gentium*

I limit myself to some suggestions that have been insufficiently elaborated and rather point to paths for future work.

[49] Boff, *Eclesiogênese*, 79.

[50] Ibid., 97f.

[51] Congar, "Les implications", 166.

[52] H. U. von Balthasar points out this christological deficit in *Test Everything: Hold Fast to What Is Good* (San Francisco: Ignatius Press, 1989), 43–47.

a. *Christocentric Eschatology*

The fundamental error of eschatologism is its subordination of Jesus' eschatology to the alleged apocalyptic horizon of his time. In a recent study "On the Concept of Christian Eschatology",[53] however, Hans Urs von Balthasar has shown how very christocentric the entire eschatolog of the New Testament basically is, even where it makes use of the language of Jewish apocalyptic. Christ's eschatology determines the views of his disciples, more in its substance than in the literary modes of expression. Let us take the "little apocalypses" of the synoptic evangelists: "If one takes an overview of the texts without any preconceptions, he will be astonished to see how many of them . . . refer to the direct effect of the presence of Jesus in the world." [54] This is not a scenario that would simply have been drawn from the world of apocalyptic images; it deals essentially with the consequences of the coming of Jesus Christ and of the *krisis* provoked by this coming. In the case of the "false prophets" (Mt 24:4 et passim), for example, it seems to be a case of some who are calling into question the uniqueness of Christ, and even the wars and the natural catastrophes (Mt 24:6–8) have a "christological motivation", since they transpose to the societal and cosmic level the separations that Jesus already provokes on the

---

[53] *Theodramatik. IV. Das Endspiel* (Einsiedeln, 1983), 14–46.
[54] Ibid., 28.

level of the family.[55] There is no "neutral" apocalyptic—apocalyptic always has Christ as its center—and
there is no serious reason to exclude the possibility that
this "christocentrism" of the New Testament eschatology ultimately arose from the consciousness that Christ
himself had of his mission, of his "hour".[56] Is it possible
to avoid the conclusion that Jesus Christ was conscious
of being himself the *eschaton*, in his mission and in his
person?

Karl Barth, who was a "consistent eschatologist" in
his *Römerbrief* (1922), altered his position totally,[57] in
order to orient eschatology once again on the mystery
of Christ: Jesus himself "is the kingdom, he was the
kingdom, and will be the kingdom, and in him exist
the entire establishment, all the salvation, all the perfection, all the joy of the kingdom. To speak precisely,
there are no 'last things': no abstract, no autonomous
'last things' apart from and alongside him who is *the*
Last." [58]

---

[55] Ibid., 31.

[56] On this, cf. the document of the International Theological Commission, "Jesu Selbst- und Sendungsbewusstsein", in *IKZ Communio* 16
(1987), 38–49.

[57] K. Barth writes in his *Kirchliche Dogmatik*, vol. III, 2, 562: "It is precisely a 'consistent' eschatology, which must look on the intervening
time between 'now' and 'once in the future' as a time of emptiness, of
nothingness, of a mere deprivation, of increasing disappointment which is
laboriously concealed, that is *not* the eschatology of New Testament
Christianity."

[58] Ibid., 589.

Once he has given back eschatology its own, definitive place in Jesus Christ as its center, Karl Barth can again discover what the older writers, both Catholic and Protestant, never lost from view: the Church is the kingdom. " 'The kingdom of God' means the lordship set up in Jesus Christ in the world, God's ruling that takes place in him. He himself is the kingdom of God. One should therefore not suppress the proposition that has often been attacked too quickly and too heedlessly in Protestant theology: the *kingdom of God* is the community." [59]

b. *"Ecclesia de Angelis"* [60]

It is impossible to understand the Church in her mystery, which can be grasped only in faith,[61] if one fails to take into account that part of the Church, of the kingdom of God, which forms above all the Church of heaven: the holy angels. In order to quicken the senses to perceive the true nature of the Church, we must continually recall this fellowship between the pilgrim Church and the saints and angels of heaven—this is the theme of chapter VII of *Lumen gentium*. When the

[59] Ibid, IV, 2, 742; cf. Carmignac, *Le mirage*, 184–88.

[60] Cf. L. Bouyer, *Die Kirche*, vol. II: *Theologie der Kirche* (Einsiedeln, 1977), in the chapter on LG 7 and 8.

[61] *Fide solum intelligimus*, says the Catechism of the Council of Trent with a view to the mystery of the Church. K. Barth mentions this with acknowledgment and agreement in *Zwischen den Zeiten*, vol. 5 (1927), 365–78.

mentions of the holy angels in the liturgy, where they
had had a central place since the Apocalypse, were reduced and made almost void of significance, was not
this an all too easy capitulation to a certain rational-
ism? [62] "The *ekklesia* of the Eucharist would then be no
mere assembly of men among themselves, but—as the
Jews already believed and affirmed in their *berakoth*—
the gathering of redeemed men with the angels who
are the first servants of their salvation, as they also were
the first to recognize the love of God and to respond
to this with praise. This corresponds also to the vision
of the Church offered us in the Christian Apocalypse:
the earthly Eucharist that is perfected and is transposed
into heaven and as it were drawn into the liturgy of
the angels." [63]

How are we to keep alive the knowledge of the invisible dimension of the Church, when her invisible
members are forgotten in our liturgical assemblies, at
which they are present? The consciousness that the angels belong to the Church has "directly the wholly
practical consequences that no one can be a prophet or
an apostle unless he has *first been a contemplative and an
intercessor* like the angels. For one cannot effectively
transmit, on the level of man or on the level of an
angel, anything that one has not first made most deeply
one's own. It is only when *agape* has taken control of
our entire being that God, thanks to the maternal grace

[62] Cf. Peterson, "Von den Engeln", n. 10.
[63] L. Bouyer, *Die Kirche*, 402.

that he wanted to communicate to his entire creation, to his entire heavenly and earthly Church, can bestow on us, if he wishes, the gift of the simple prophetic testimony or of the apostolic mission in the name of his Son. In this sense, the bishops ought to be the 'angels of the Church', according to the ancient interpretation of the Apocalypse (cf. Rev 2:1, 8, 12, 18, etc.)." [64]

c. *Maria-Ecclesia*

Although the identity between Church and kingdom has its basis in Christ, there is no higher concretization of this identity for the Church than the Mother of God. It would not be possible to assert this identity if its only basis were Christ, the Head of the Church, and there was no real perfect correspondence on the side of the members of the Church. One may justly say that, if Mary did not exist in the Church, then there would be a distance between the Church and the kingdom, because of the presence of sinners in the Church (cf. note 25). But "in the most Blessed Virgin the Church has already reached that perfection whereby she exists without spot or wrinkle (cf. Eph 5:27)" (LG 65). In Mary, the most perfect member of the Church, we are able to contemplate the Church's true nature. Thus, "by contemplating Mary's mysterious holiness, by imitating her love and faithfully carrying out the Father's will, the

[64] Ibid., 403.

Church too herself becomes a mother through receiving the Word of God in faith" (LG 64). If Mary did not exist in the Church, one could not speak with full correctness of the Church's motherhood.

"*The Church's motherhood is something that already exists in reality only because the Church has found here her anticipated perfection*: the highest created holiness in a unique communication with Christ's own holiness, who communicates it to her who is not only the mother of us all, but is first of all his own mother." [65] In Mary, the Council wanted to display to us the sign of the Church but also the Church's reality: both the eschatological character of the earthly, pilgrim Church and her inseparable unity with the Church of heaven. "As the Mother of Jesus, already glorified with body and soul in heaven, is the image and the beginning of the Church, which will be perfected in the world to come, so she also shines here on earth in the intermediary time until the day of the Lord comes (cf. 2 Pt 3:10) as a sign of sure hope and of consolation to the people of God on its pilgrim way" (LG 68).

[65] Ibid., 406.

Chapter IV

THE CHURCH BETWEEN HOPE IN
LIFE AFTER DEATH
AND RESPONSIBILITY FOR LIFE
HERE ON EARTH

Many people today are worried about a certain politici-
zation of the churches or of some groups in the
churches. The following fragmentary reflections are an
attempt to make a small contribution toward clearing up
these worries. It is not a question here of immediately
practical reflections on how the relationship between
Church and politics is to be ordered, to what extent the
Church ought and may "get involved" in politics, or
where the mutual boundaries and the common areas lie.
Switzerland is a country in which Church and state,
religious groups and political groups live in an unusually
harmonious relationship. One look at today's world
suffices to show that this harmony does not exist in
broad sections of the community of peoples. Today, attacks by the power of the state in the area of the freedom of religious groups are the principal cause of
disturbance to the relationship between Church and
state. But one is made uneasy also by attacks in the

99

other direction, when on occasion claim is laid to political competence on the basis of religious arguments, or the prestige of ecclesiastical authority is adduced as a significant political factor.

In what follows, we deal with very fundamental questions, which may appear to some to be insufficiently practical. But I believe that it is worthwhile and indeed necessary to pose the question whether the relationship between Church and politics is not *always* a relationship fraught with tension. This is what history indicates. The question is only whether this tension is good and useful, or harmful and reprehensible. What direction ought the Church to take? If she concentrates on the hope of life after death as her own proper task, she is accused of a lack of responsibility for life here on earth. If she becomes more involved in temporal affairs, she is criticized for forgetting her orientation to eternal life. What direction ought the Church to take?

We shall investigate this question in three steps.

1. Jean-Jacques Rousseau's thesis of the socially damaging character of Christianity will introduce us to the question by showing us its coordinates.

2. Under the heading "No One Can Serve Two Masters", we discuss the central question of the source of the perennial conflict between Church and politics.

3. In the concluding section, we attempt to bring into play a third entity that is usually forgotten and tends to be overlooked.

1. Jean-Jacques Rousseau's Thesis of the Socially Damaging Character of Christianity

In the concluding chapter of his *Contrat social*, dealing with the *religion civile*, Jean-Jacques Rousseau says of the Christian religion: "Far from winning the hearts of the citizens for the state, it removes them from it, as from all earthly things. I know nothing that is more actively opposed to the social spirit." [1] Rousseau asserts that Christianity is hostile to the state, and he justifies this assertion by affirming that Christianity is a purely spiritual religion "which is occupied only with heavenly things: the native land of the Christian is not of this world." Rousseau holds that, if Christians are unable to be good citizens, this is based in the intentions of Jesus himself: "Jesus came in order to set up a spiritual kingdom on earth; thereby the theological system was separated from the political system, and this in turn meant that the state ceased to be *one* state, and that inherent tensions emerged, which have never since ceased to agitate the Christian peoples." The outcome is "a continuous struggle between the jurisdictions . . . , which has made any reasonable civil order impossible in the Christian states". The effect of Christianity is that men now have "two legislations, two sovereigns, two native lands", so that they are subjected to "antithetical obliga-

[1] *Du Contrat social*, IV, 8; quoted from the German translation by E. Koch in J.-J. Rousseau, *Sozialphilosophische und politische Schriften* (Munich, 1981), 386.

tions": this is why the Christian can never be simultaneously pious and a good citizen. Rousseau holds, accordingly, that such a religion, which gives men a double
citizenship, the earthly and the heavenly, cannot be integrated into society (*insociable*).[2]

Rousseau's thesis is not new, but it gave a program-
matic and effective expression to the problem that is at
issue here: the Christians' hope of life after death makes
them useless in terms of taking responsibility for life
here on earth. Since their hearts are attached to heaven,
they cannot love the earth, and since their Lord is in
heaven, they will never belong wholly to the lords of
this earth. Rousseau asserts that Christianity is radically
contrary to the *esprit social*. If we look more closely at
this accusation, we see that it contains in reality two
mutually contradictory charges.

The first charge runs as follows: Christianity weakens
responsibility for society, since it turns men into cow-
ardly slaves who think only of how they are to attain
paradise and are not interested in the well-being of society: "He is little concerned whether everything here
below is in a good or a bad condition." "And ultimately, what does it matter whether one is a free man
or a slave in this vale of tears? The main point is that
one should attain paradise." One could almost fancy it
was Nietzsche speaking: "The true Christians are
created in order to be slaves."[3] Because Christians at-

2 Ibid., 382–86.
3 Ibid., 386f.

tach too little value to this short life, they lack the
strength to commit themselves actively to improving
life on earth.

The second charge seems to run contrary to the first:
under the disguise of their weakness, Christians are in
reality *de vrais rebelles*. They make a hypocritical show of
submissiveness, but they are merely waiting for the opportunity to revolt, so that they themselves may usurp
the power to which they pretended to submit. The pagans were not mistaken to think thus, and this was also
the reason for the persecution of Christians.[4] Christians
are secretly rebels against the state!

How does Rousseau arrive at such contradictory ac-
cusations in his rejection of Christianity ("The Christian
law is basically damaging rather than useful to the
strong constitution of a state")?[5] We find the answer to
this question in the solution to the problem that Rousseau praises. He holds that Thomas Hobbes was the
only one to have identified both the ill and the remedy:
one must "reunite both heads of the eagle and bring
everything back to the political unity without which
neither state nor government will ever be well constituted".[6] "Everything that lacerates societal unity is useless",[7] and this is precisely what Christianity does. This
is why it must be replaced by the *religion civile*, which

4 Ibid., 382.
5 Ibid., 384.
6 Ibid.
7 Ibid., 385.

alone guarantees the unity of society. The double eagle has one head too many—that of the religious authority. If it is not willing to identify itself with the principle of political unity, then the only solution left is to cut off the superfluous head. Rousseau's program of the *Contrat social* is militant, and although it makes a law of tolerance, it is totalitarian in its innermost depths. This was seen after 1789 at the latest, when heads began to roll in the name of the *religion civile*.

Why have we made this excursion into Rousseau's political "*rêverie*"?[8] For the simple reason that Rousseau formulated very clearly the problem about which we shall speak in what follows. One could make many historical and theological objections to his arguments, but this does not alter the *fact* that Rousseau's theses, in one form or another, have been cropping up continually since the beginnings of Christianity. The accusation that Christianity is hostile to the state and socially damaging, that it destroys the unity of society, is as old as Christianity itself, and one may correctly deduce from this that this charge does not merely have its origin in the wickedness or ignorance of the enemies of Christianity but has its justification in the very essence of the matter. We must now attempt to get to the bottom of this, for what we have here is one of the structurally significant foundations of the relationship between Church and politics, of Christianity and society.

[8] Thus F. Bouchardy in the introduction (p. 9) to his edition of the *Contrat social* (Paris, 1946).

2. "No One Can Serve Two Masters" (Mt 6:24)

Deus major est, non Imperatores ("God is the greater One, not the emperors")—this cry of an early Christian martyr indicates concisely and clearly the source of the conflicts.[9] Such a statement is unthinkable in the classical, pre-Christian world. Religion and state are coterminous, so that it was not possible for any antithesis to exist between god and ruler, since the ruler was the god's representative. In the pre-Christian sphere, man can be the citizen of only one city, the city of his gods, of his fathers, in which religion and society are identical. This was true even of the Roman Empire, that conglomeration of many peoples that assimilated all the cults and integrated them into one civic religion. It was not possible for any conflict to arise in the pantheon of classical Rome between the gods and the emperors, since the world of the gods and the world of men together formed one common house (so to speak). It is only when one bears this in mind that he will understand why the classical world had no idea what to make of the Christians' attitude vis-à-vis the state. The pagan philosopher Celsus, toward the end of the second century, points out to the Christians: "You say that it is not possible for one and the same man to serve several lords: but surely that is *the language of rebellion*, the lan-

[9] The Martyr Emeritus in the *Acta Saturnini* 11; German text in K. Gamber, *Sie gaben Zeugnis. Authentische Berichte über Märtyrer der Frühkirche* (Regensburg, 1982), 96.

guage of people who shut themselves off from other men as with a wall and tear themselves loose from everything." [10]

Because Christians refuse to give cultic honor to the emperor and wish to serve only *one* master, namely, *their own*, their behavior counts as rebellion. But since the exclusiveness of their cult for their Lord leaves no space for the other gods, they are accused of godlessness, of atheism.[11]

Christ brought something radically new into the world. With one word, he separated God and the emperor: "Give to Caesar what belongs to Caesar, and to God what belongs to God" (Mt 22:21). With this word, he "dedivinizes" the emperor, and at the same time he indicates the obedience that is owed precisely to this emperor. When he stands before Pontius Pilate as one accused, he tells the representative of the emperor, "Yes, I am a king", but says at the same time: "My kingdom is not of this world", and when Pilate refers to his own power, Jesus does not dispute this, but replies: "You would not have any power over me, if it had not been given to you from above" (Jn 18:36, 37; 19:11).

What is new about Christianity is not so much its doctrine, as Christ himself. What is new in the Chris-

---

[10] In Origen, *Contra Celsum* VIII, 2; quoted from H. Rahner, *Kirche und Staat im frühen Christentum. Dokumente aus acht Jahrhunderten und ihre Deutung* (Munich, 1961), 22. This book, written during the Second World War ("when the struggle between state and Church was fought out in Germany", p. 11), is the best introduction I know to this problem.

[11] Cf. Justin Martyr (c. 150), *Apol.* 1, 6, 1; 46, 3; *Dial.* 108, 2, etc.

tians' behavior is their relationship to Christ. From his Resurrection onward, Christ is honored and addressed by the Christians as *Kyrios* (Lord). They pray, as he himself taught them to pray, for the coming of his kingdom, the kingdom of God. It was inevitable that their belonging to Christ should appear to be a rivalry to the emperor, who himself laid claim to the title of *Kyrios*. The emperor cannot tolerate the situation where citizens of his realm claim to have chosen another than himself as their highest Lord. The governor appeals to the aged Polycarp to renounce his allegiance to Christ and to swear by the *genius* of the emperor. Polycarp's reply demonstrates the whole significance of the conflict: "For eighty-six years I have served him [Christ], and he has never done me any wrong. How could I now blaspheme against my King and Savior?" [12]

What is new about Christianity is this unconditional belonging to Christ, with the consequence that Christians have their rights as citizens in the kingdom of Christ or, as Paul says, "in the heavens" (Phil 3:20). Their right as citizens in the kingdom of Christ is more important to them than their earthly right, and they are willing to yield this up, if necessary. This will be the attitude of Franz Jägerstätter, the Austrian farmer executed in 1943 who justified his solitary decision to refuse military service under Hitler on the ground that he could not serve at one and the same time the king-

12 Martyrdom of Saint Polycarp, IX, 3.

dom (*Reich*) of Christ and the Third Reich.[13] This attitude brings a yeast of division into a world that is self-
satisfied and does not tolerate an additional belonging to
another world. Thus it is not by chance that the early
Christians feel themselves to be foreigners and pilgrims
in this world, since their native land is with Christ "in
the heavens" and they are en route to the "coming"
city (Heb 13:14). A hymn puts it thus: "We are but
guests on earth, and wander without rest toward the
eternal homeland, bearing many kinds of burdens." The
marvelous Letter to Diognetus from the second century
speaks the same language: "They [Christians] dwell
each in his native land, but only as resident aliens; they
carry out all the tasks of a citizen and endure all the
burdens like foreigners; every foreign land is a native
land to them, and every native land is a foreign land to
them." [14] "They live on earth, but they are citizens in
heaven." [15]

It has repeatedly been asserted that early Christians
lived in an intense hope of life after death: they awaited
so keenly the imminent irruption of God's sovereignty
and the imminent return of Christ that there was no
place at all left for an interest in this world, its miseries,
and its needs. It would be only the failure of these
events to materialize, and the sobering disappointment

[13] Cf. my essay "Franz Jägerstätter. Ein Zeugnis", in *IKZ Communio* 9
(1980), 271–78.
[14] Letter to Diognetus v, 5.
[15] Ibid., v, 9.

caused by the simple continuation of the course of history, that moved Christians to establish themselves as a stable earthly fellowship and to organize themselves as a structured Church. This schematic view of history, which appeared in the nineteenth century, is false, because it sees only one side of the reality (cf. Chapter 3 above). It is indeed doubtless true that the first generations of Christians still lived in an intense expectation of the imminent return of Christ (cf. 1 Th 4:15–17 and other texts), but this is only one side of the matter. It does not suffice to explain why Christianity, from its early days and again and again throughout its entire history, became a source of conflict in society. A community that does nothing but look with yearning to the life beyond death is scarcely likely to be considered a danger to the existing order of things, especially if (like Christianity) it obliges its members to behave peacefully, justly, and humbly.[16] If Christians merely looked on this world as a waiting room in which one watched for the signal to depart for the heavenly Jerusalem, there would be no cause to think of them as anything more than mere mixed-up dreamers.

---

[16] H. de Lubac, whose book *Die Kirche. Eine Betrachtung*, translated by H. U. von Balthasar (Einsiedeln, 1968), has given valuable stimulus to our reflections here, quotes a commentator on Hobbes (J. Vialatoux, *La cité de Hobbes, théorie de l'Etat totalitaire* [1935], 168): "Will a king who learns that his subject awaits another king only at the end of the world, be so crazy as to punish him for this with death? It is enough for earthly kings that they reign fully each over his own kingdom."

Jesus Christ, however, left behind quite a different charge from that of an inactive waiting around. He did indeed confess before Pilate that his kingdom was not of this world, but his final charge to his disciples runs: "All authority in heaven and *on earth* has been given to me. Go therefore and make all peoples my disciples, and baptize them in the name of the Father and of the Son and of the Holy Spirit, and teach them to observe all that I have commanded you! And behold, I am with you all days, even to the end of the world" (Mt 28:18–20).

These mighty words explain why a conflict *had* to arise about Christianity. The future, heavenly kingdom of God is at the same time a present reality. Christians affirm that their *Kyrios* is *already* Lord of heaven *and* of earth. They believe that they are charged with the task of making all peoples, all men, disciples of Jesus and of bringing them to live and to act in keeping with Jesus' ideas. The early Church cries out with yearning for the speedy return of the Lord ("Maranatha", 1 Cor 16:22; cf. Rev 22:20), but she acts no less decisively to win men for Christ "from all nations and tribes and peoples and tongues" (Rev 7:9) already *now*. The kingdom of God is "eschatological". It belongs to the end time, yet the end time has already begun in Christ. His kingdom is not *of* this world, but it comes *into* this world. For where men become his disciples, they form not a group thrown together by chance but a structured fellowship that is constituted in a visible manner and displays in its fundamental structure an organic continuity with its origin. The Church's fellowship is neither a merely secular religious grouping nor a purely spiritual community: it is neither an exclusively visible Church nor an exclusively invisible Church. It is both at one and the same time, and in an inseparable fashion, earthly and heavenly Church, a structured society and a spiritual fellowship.[17]

Here lies the deepest root of the problem that Rousseau has exposed acutely. This is the new element in relation to the pre-Christian societal systems: religion and society are no longer coterminous; the gods and heroes no longer form a unified cosmos. Rousseau's dream of closing this gaping hole again and reestablishing the total *"Unité sociale"* could only lead to totalitarianism. It is no longer possible to remove the dualism between Church and state, between the claim of the "earthly city" (*civitas terrena*) and the "city of God" (*civitas Dei*). Christians are "citizens of two worlds". But this means that the conflict that determines in ever new variants the mutual relationship of these two worlds is "programmed in advance". The demands of the *civitas terrena* and the claims of the *civitas Dei* cannot be distributed between life on earth and life in heaven, or the material and the spiritual spheres, or politics and religion. For the conflict is inscribed in the heart of man, who must endeavor to be a good citizen of the

[17] Cf. Vatican Council II, Constitution on the Church, *Lumen gentium*, no. 8.

civitas terrena without denying his belonging to the *civitas Dei*. Henri de Lubac has given a penetrating description of this unavoidable conflict between Church and society:

> Thus there arises from the very nature of things a rivalry between the two, an almost unceasing struggle. Each complains of the "encroachments" of the other. Nothing is less secure or more exposed to danger than their equilibrium. Even when men on both sides search for a settlement, it is only seldom that the two legislations find a full harmony. Scarcely has one conflict been laid to rest, when a new conflict breaks out, muffled or fierce, petty or tragic.
>
> Twenty centuries suffice to attest that it is virtually impossible to find the equilibrium. At one time, it is the state that persecutes; at another time, men of the Church usurp for themselves the rights of the state in one or another sphere. No form of separation or of unification is without its specific disadvantages. And the most perfect symbioses are likewise those that are most to be feared. The best turns most easily into the worst. Often, one does not know which authority is enslaved to the other: whether it is the Church that lords it over the world, or the world that has forced its way into the Church. In order to escape from the dualism, one falls into some kind of monism, and if the intermingling is openly recognized, new antitheses arise. . . . In the mildest cases, a permanent "mutual superiority" holds sway. The existence of the individual thus becomes more complicated in every sphere—if indeed he is not precipitated into se-

rious conflicts. The believer and the citizen are torn
asunder in the innermost sphere of one and the same
person.[18]

Thus Rousseau seems to be right in laying this conflict
to the charge of Christianity: "Everything that lacerates
societal unity is useless: all institutions that bring man
into a state of self-contradiction are useless."[19] This accusation is repeated up to our own days. Attempts have
been made up to the present to resolve the tension by
prescribing a unity for society and an identity for the individual in which no space remains for this conflict. All
totalitarian societal forms, whether atheistic, theocratic,
or nationalistic, aim for such a unity. The experiences
of our century justify one in doubting whether this
unity is in keeping with human nature. We must ur-
gently ask the opposite question: Whether the conflict
indicated here is not healthier than the attempts to exclude it? Perhaps it is good and necessary for the tension
between Church and society to exist and for the individual to be obliged to support this tension in himself
and for society as a whole to support it and to fight out
this battle again and again. For it is certainly possible
that the equilibrium between Church and society and
between the claims of both—an equilibrium so difficult
to establish—is a positive challenge that is fundamen-

[18] De Lubac, *Die Kirche*, 143f. The article "Kirche und Staat" in the
Staatslexikon (ed. by the Görres-Gesellschaft), vol. 4 (Freiburg, 1959),
cols. 991–1050, gives a good overview.

[19] *Du Contrat social*, IV, 8.

tally beneficial to the individual man who must unite in himself the claims of both the Church and the society to which he belongs.

The decisive question, however, is: What kind of unity will remove the conflict between Church and society? In what does the reconciliation of the antitheses consist? It is not *possible* for any attempt to bring about the reconciliation of all antitheses and thereby the total harmony of man with himself and with his world in a political, societal entity (state, nation, classless society) to bear any other form than that of totalitarianism. Christianity has brought a decisive *liberation* here: the kingdom of God is not of this world; the sphere of the reconciliation of all antitheses is not to be found *within* history; perfect unity lies ahead of us, not as a utopian horizon in history but as a promise beyond history. Not even the Church is the place where all antitheses are reconciled, and as long as the Church is "in the condition of a pilgrim", she will never know perfect unity (or the perfect reunification of all Christians!). The pilgrim Church is not yet the perfected kingdom of God.[20] This, however, also means that the ultimate goal of man cannot lie in *this* world. Thomas Aquinas has formulated this with Latin clarity in view of the question that concerns us here: "*Homo non ordinatur ad communitatem politicam secundum se totum et secundum omnia sua, . . . sed totum quod homo est, et quod potest et habet, or-*

[20] Cf. nos. 3, 5, and 48 of *Lumen gentium* and Chapter 3 above.

dinatum est ad Deum." (No man belongs *wholly* to the state, to the political community. Man belongs *wholly* only to God, to whom he is wholly oriented with all that he is, can do, and has.)[21]

This does not mean that there exists no orientation of man to society. Thomas Aquinas, and with him the entire social doctrine of the Church, emphasizes that every man, as a member of the community, is oriented to the good of the totality of the community.[22] But this does not mean that man is utterly absorbed into the community.

We may perhaps not realize so clearly today what a liberating power has lain and still lies in this distinction and in its practical consequences, since—at least in free countries—the separation of secular and spiritual authority has become something we take for granted. Naturally, we owe this distinction, as well as the acknowledgment of the freedom of conscience that is linked to it, to Christianity's fundamental conviction that no man belongs *wholly* to the state, the nation, or the "collective", but can and may belong *wholly* only to him who is his Creator and his goal.

We can make this clear through two examples from the early Christian period, which both have great relevance for today. It appears that classical medicine attached little importance to the life of the newborn.

[21] *Summa Theologiae* I–II, q. 21, a. 4 ad 3.

[22] Ibid., II–II, q. 58 c.; cf. on this J. Maritain, *Primauté du spirituel* (Paris, 1927), and *Humanisme intégral* (Paris, 1937).

Hippocrates poses the question of which children one ought to bring up (and this presupposes that it was not taken for granted that *all* should be kept alive). Cicero holds that the death of a child is something that can be borne with serenity. The wise Seneca, indeed, thinks it reasonable to drown sickly and weak children. Tacitus is surprised at the Jewish custom of not killing any newborns. Christians clearly prohibit abortion from the very outset.[23] They respect every life, even that of the newborn. This attitude can be understood only as the expression of the fact that human life is not evaluated primarily in terms of its value or lack of value for the totality of society but is seen as the life of a human *person* who is entirely oriented to God from the first moment of his existence and is thus not available to other people to dispose of. Even today, the only way to justify the protection of unborn or handicapped life is on the basis of the inviolable dignity of the spiritual person created by God and oriented to God. It is, in my view, an illusion to seek to justify this inviolability on exclusively societal grounds. It is widely taken for granted today that "social indications" are acceptable grounds for abortion, and this shows how close we have come to the view of classical paganism that the

[23] Cf. R. Etienne, "La conscience médicale antique et la vie des enfants", in *Annales de démographie historique* (1973), the fascicle on "Enfant et Société", quoted from R. Pernoud, *La femme au temps des cathédrales* (Paris, 1980), 23f.

education of children is the art "of deciding which newborn children are worth being brought up".[24]

A second example is the emancipation of woman in Christian antiquity. Régine Pernoud has pointed out that the possibility of choosing an unmarried life for the sake of Christ brought a liberation of woman unheard of in classical times. By deciding to belong to Christ alone, Christian women withdraw themselves from the *patria potestas* that was taken for granted in antiquity. The woman or girl no longer belongs wholly to her father and family. In this free choice, she proves herself to be an inviolable person, in her dignity that God has bestowed on her.[25] Various accounts or legends of martyrs from the early Church show us that this new freedom was sometimes also paid for with these women's lives.

The double citizenship of which Rousseau complains, introduced into the world by Christianity, signifies de facto conflict and crisis. It brings a ferment of disorder into society. Not everyone is pleased with this, and so Christianity is repeatedly accused of dissidence and of secret rebellion. But thus an invaluable ferment of freedom is introduced at the same time, a ferment that defends again and again, in a unique manner, the inalienable dignity of man against every form of degradation.[26]

[24] Soranos of Ephesus, quoted by R. Etienne, "La conscience".

[25] R. Pernoud, *La femme*, 24–31.

[26] There is an immense body of writing on the theme of Christianity and human rights. It suffices to refer to the document of the International

3. The Kingdom of God, Society, and the Problem of Evil

What we have said up to this point can give the impression that the conflict criticized by Rousseau, which de facto appears again and again, between the heavenly citizenship and the earthly is caused by the clash of two unreconciled and irreconcilable worlds here. Are "Church" and "world", *civitas Dei* and *civitas terrena*, antagonistic entities, essentially hostile to one another? This tendency has existed again and again in the long history of the doctrine of the two kingdoms.[27] Its newest variant, which is still potently effective at the present day, is the view held by the so-called political theology that the Church is something like the "institutionalized critique of society".[28] We hear also of the "critically liberating function of the Church" in relation to society, giving the impression that a society that is permanently criticized in this way is ultimately a negative entity that must be fundamentally called into question. Indeed, the hallmark of this criticism is that society in all its spheres (economics, culture, defense) is

Theological Commission, "La dignité et les droits de la personne humaine", in *La Documentation Catholique*, no. 1893, April 7, 1985, 383–91.

[27] Cf. E. Gilson, *Les métamorphoses de la Cité de Dieu* (Louvain and Paris, 1952), and de Lubac, "Political Augustinianism", in *Theological Fragments* (San Francisco: Ignatius Press, 1989), 235–86.

[28] On this, see the critical confrontation with the theses of J. B. Metz, the protagonist of this new "political theology", in H. Maier, *Kritik der politischen Theologie* (Einsiedeln, 1970).

continually told it must have a "bad conscience": not because of particular abuses and wrong attitudes but fundamentally and universally. It is not the abusive practices of banks that are criticized but their very existence; not this or that measure taken in the defense of a country but the very existence of this defense. Behind this criticism, which likes to call itself "prophetic", there lies in reality a kind of "political millenarianism" [29] that, in the name of a future "paradisal" society, rejects and "demonizes" the existing society *en bloc*, demanding that it be overthrown by revolution.

We have presented the relationship between Church and society, between *civitas Dei* and *civitas terrena*, up to now as full of tensions. This picture would be one-sided if we failed now to add precision by means of a new element: *the problem of evil.*

Two basic temptations run through the history of the relationship between Church and society, between religion and politics in the West: we can call these, somewhat summarily, the *naturalistic* and the *Manichaean* temptations. The latter sees the two entities as mutually

[29] We refer here to the monumental work of H. de Lubac: *La postérité spirituelle de Joachime de Flore,* bk. I, *de Joachim à Schelling;* bk. II, *de Saint Simon à nos jours* (Paris and Namur, 1978 and 1981); cf. also the books by A. Besançon, *Les origines intellectuelles du Léninisme* (Paris, 1977) and *La falsification du bien, Soloviev et Orwell* (Paris, 1985); cf. also J. M. Garrigues, *L'Eglise, la société libre et le communisme,* Collection "Commentaire Juillard" (Paris, 1984). Cf. also J. Pieper's book *Hope and History* (San Francisco: Ignatius Press, 1994), which is important for our subject as a whole.

hostile by their very nature: the "world" is evil, only the "kingdom of light" is good, and an implacable conflict exists between these two. Evil is located on one side exclusively: the world, society, politics, etc.; the good lies only on the spiritual, heavenly, or future side. The "naturalistic" temptation consists in denying the problem of evil, declaring it to be the "so-called evil" (Konrad Lorenz), which in reality is nothing other than the play of forces according to the blind necessities of nature, in which there are conquerors and conquered but not good and evil. This is the world-view in which the highest laws are the "struggle for life" and the "survival of the fittest". It is the world-view of Darwin and all his disciples, while the "Manichaean" temptation is that of the Marxist world-view. Jacques Maritain has characterized these two tendencies as typically "right" and "left". The "left" temptation is to hate that which *is* and to dream of that which ought to be ("*Il n'y a de beau que ce qui n'est pas*", said Rousseau): the "right" temptation is to see only that which de facto is and to reject as daydreams that which ought to be.[30]

Charles Journet (d. 1975), surely one of the most significant spiritual figures of modern Church history, recognized with rare clarity as a theologian and a vigilant observer of the contemporary intellectual and political scene the great dangers of these two temptations, especially in the dramatic events of the 1930s and 1940s:

[30] Cf. J. Maritain, *Lettre sur l'Independance* (Paris, 1935) and *Le Paysan de la Garonne* (Paris, 1966), 38–43.

the dangers of political ideologies that close themselves completely to the claim of the kingdom of God, and the dangers of religious ideologies that want to change the kingdom of God directly into a political-revolutionary force. Both dangers come from a false view of the problem of evil. Cardinal Journet pointed out again and again that, according to the Christian vision, society, "*la cité de l'homme*", belongs to the natural order, the order of creation, which in itself is good and possesses its relative autonomy, its own positive values, and its own finality: the "common good" (*bonum commune*). Culture, science, economics, and politics have their positive values, which cannot simply be identified with man's ultimate goal, which can only be God—and this goal gives man an orientation to an eternal determination that lies beyond all temporal values. The kingdom of God, the *civitas Dei*, is this ultimate goal, which is already present in the Church and is to penetrate and reshape all temporal values, without calling their autonomy into question. The great merit of the Second Vatican Council is that it defined the relationship of Church and society in this sense. The Church renounces all theocratic claims to a *directly* political or societal power. She wants to be a *ferment* in society by promoting all that is good, affirming all positive values, and helping to keep these values open to the ultimate goal of man. This is why the Council repeatedly speaks of the *dialogue* between the Church and the world. What then is the source of the antagonisms that so often weigh down upon this relationship?

It is not because of the *nature* of human society that
conflicts between "Church" and "world" keep on aris-
ing. Charles Journet speaks, with Augustine, of a third
reality, of which people do not like to speak today: the
civitas diaboli, the power of evil.[31] Although no period
of history has known such a massive number of external
manifestations of evil as our century, an astonishing
blindness exists on this topic. The Council speaks a
beneficial clear language here: "The whole of man's
history has been the story of dour combat with the
powers of evil, stretching, so our Lord tells us (Mt
24:13; 13:24–30 and 36–43), from the very dawn of history until the last day. Finding himself in the midst of
the battlefield man has to struggle to do what is right,
and it is at great cost to himself, and aided by God's
grace, that he succeeds in achieving his own inner in-
tegrity."[32]

Let us attempt to draw some conclusions in the light
of this clarification, which is certainly not comfortable
but is thereby all the more healthy.

1. It must be said, against all utopias, that there is no
paradise on earth. We are here only as pilgrims; the goal
of our life is not here but "there", in God's eternal
kingdom. The provisional character of *all* earthly reali-

---

[31] Charles Journet, "Les trois cités: celle de Dieu, celle de l'homme,
celle du diable", in *Nova et Vetera* 33 (1958), 25–48; cf. also the text of a
speech on this subject that Cardinal Journet made during the Council,
published in *La Liberté*, April 15, 1985 (p. 5).

[32] Pastoral Constitution *Gaudium et spes*, no. 37, 2.

zations, even the greatest and most beautiful, is something we must never forget. Perfect justice, total peace, and completely successful identity do not exist in this life. To accept this frees politics from the compulsion to bring about the impossible by forcible means; it frees society from the penetrating critic that wants *everything* to be perfect, already here and now.

2. Against all resignation, however, it must also be said that (relative) joy, (relative) success, and (relative) justice can and should exist already in this life. For the Christian, heaven is already on earth, in a certain sense. For where he attempts in this time, with all its provisional character, to create space for love, to lend a voice to justice, to live peace, there—even in the midst of great deficiencies and miseries—something of heaven can already be sensed on earth.

3. Against all utopias of the "left" and against all resignation of the "right", the Christian knows that the decisive struggle is not a "class struggle" or a "struggle for existence" but the continuous struggle against the power of evil, against the forces of pride, of arrogance, of hatred, through which "the prince of this world" (Jn 12:31) builds up his kingdom and his lordship, and which are the ultimate source of all injustice and all evil. The Gospel speaks here with an unsurpassable clarity. The victory over the power of evil can be won only through *sacrifice* and *renunciation*. No one can be spared from *suffering* or from death, which sets a boundary to all our striving. If we become aware once more

that we are given a short time in which to fight this struggle, and if we never forget that we are to find and to take the path to eternal life in this brief time span of our life but can also fail to take this path or lose it,[33] then we shall "make the best use of the time" (Eph 5:16), knowing how serious time is, and we shall "live sober, righteous, and pious lives in the present world" (Titus 2:12).

True "responsibility for life here on earth" is generated only by the genuine "hope in life after death". But the opposite is true likewise: only responsibility for eternal life gives the right joy in this life: "responsibility for life after death" generates the genuine "hope for this life here on earth".

---

[33] On this subject, cf. also my essay "Hoffnung über den Tod hinaus—Einübung des Lebens", in A. H. Graf Henckel-Donnersmark and S. Graf Bethlen (eds.), *Vom menschlichen Sterben und vom Sinn des Todes* (Freiburg: Herder, 1983), 133–48, and Chapter 6 in this book.

Chapter V

REINCARNATION
AND CHRISTIAN FAITH

There can be no question that the doctrine of reincarnation finds astonishingly many adherents in "old Europe" today: statistical investigations speak of a quarter of the European population. A flood of books, periodicals, television programs, and lectures popularize the idea. Why is this belief attractive to so many people? Is it the feeling that this earthly life—despite the fact that it has been considerably lengthened—is much too brief to bear the weight of a unique and definitive significance? Is it the often oppressive impression that so many factors conditioned by society and environment limit our freedom that we cannot arrive at a definitive free decision? Or is it the sense that one cannot construct anything on grace in a society built on achievements—though only grace could give the fragments of our short life on earth a secure place in the totality of eternal perfection?

It will be difficult to give *one* answer: the phenomenon has too many layers and is too diffuse to be reduced to one common denominator. But one thing must be noted as an amazing phenomenon: in these countries, reincarnation, where it is believed in, is mostly an *image of hope*. This is quite different from the religions of East Asia, for which reincarnation is precisely the opposite of hope. Whereas everything there aims at *liberation* from the cycle of rebirths, in the West the prospect of reincarnation appears as an opportunity for gradual self-realization and higher development. Accordingly, whereas the Christian path of salvation can be proclaimed in Asia as redemption from the constraint of rebirths, the doctrine of reincarnation presents itself among us more and more as the alternative path of salvation, positing in place of the Christian hope of an eternal life given us by grace, rebirths as the path of gradual self-redemption.

In what follows, I wish to sketch an answer to two questions, although I am aware that this does not clarify *all* the questions that are involved here.

1. What position did the ancient Church take on the doctrine of reincarnation? One is told again and again that the early Church was "more open" here and that it was only gradually that the Church began to reject reincarnation.

2. Why has the Church from the very outset rejected the doctrine of the transmigration of souls? I shall attempt to show that this happened, not out of an anxious drawing of boundary lines but out of the positive certainty of faith that Jesus Christ, as *the* path to salvation, has fulfilled and perfected beyond all ex-

pectation everything that reincarnations could ever "bring".

1. What Position Did Early Christianity Take on Reincarnation?

The doctrine of the transmigration of souls was certainly not foreign to the world in which Christianity came into being, but it was not at all something universally acknowledged and accepted. On the contrary, it was an exception, and jokes were commonly made about it. Already Aristotle called "the fantasy of the Pythagoreans", according to which "any soul at all entered any body at all", "absurd" (*atopon*). For Aristotle, "each body possesses its own form and figure". The myth of metempsychosis sounds "as if someone were to say that architecture makes use of flutes. For in reality, each art must employ its own instruments, and in the same way the soul must have its own body." [1] In Aristotle, this criticism is motivated by a rational analysis of the relationship between soul and body. Since the soul is the "form" of the body, one particular soul can be united only with one particular body. The criticism of the doctrine of the transmigration of souls does not always reach the same high level as in Aristotle. One finds it in satire, e.g., in Lucian, who makes jokes about the reembodiments of Pythagoras: "Instantly I became a

[1] Aristotle, *On the Soul* 1, 3 (407b).

king, then a beggar, then a satrap, a horse, a jackdaw, a frog, and a thousand other things—I will not now delay by listing them all. Finally I became a cockerel, something I have repeatedly been." [2] Reincarnation was thus not at all universally accepted in the Greco-Roman world at the period of Christianity's beginnings, and Christianity from the outset was ranged decisively on the side of those who reject this doctrine. The rejection is unanimous and universal, without even the shadow of a compromise. Naturally, one must give an explanation to this fact, which is obvious to everyone who has studied this dossier. Early Christianity was not slow to take note of everything in the classical philosophers that could somehow or other be united to the Christian Faith. Why did this category never include reincarnation?

Let us listen to the explanation offered by Gregory of Nyssa in his *Life of Moses*. Zipporah, Moses' wife, is the image of the profane culture the usefulness of which is not rejected by Gregory; only, one must purify it from all foreign elements. The circumcision of Moses' son, which Zipporah carries out (Ex 4:24–26), signifies the removal of "all that is damaging and impure" from profane culture. "For alongside all the fruit of wisdom in the sciences, there clings something like flesh and foreskin: once this has been removed, what remains is the Israelite nobility. Thus, for example, the immortality of

[2] Lucian, *The Cockerel*, 20; cf. the similar remarks by the Christian philosopher Hermias: PG 6, 1169–72.

the soul is attested by pagan philosophy too; this is a genuine shoot. But the idea that the soul wanders from body to body and itself crosses over from the rational nature to the irrational—that is the fleshly and alien foreskin." [3] A powerful expression of the early Christian attitude vis-à-vis the doctrine of reincarnation!

Let us hear a further witness: Origen, who lived more than a hundred years before Gregory and was so much admired by him. Origen features without fail in the whole of the immense literature on reincarnation as the chief witness for an alleged positive attitude of early Christian theology to reincarnation. We shall see the real nature of this testimony. Let us begin by quoting a passage of his work *Against Celsus*. Celsus, a pagan philosopher, accuses the Christians of being like people who promise healing to the sick but keep them from consulting truly competent doctors because they are afraid that their own ignorance would be shown up by these doctors. For Celsus, it goes without saying that these qualified doctors are the (pagan) philosophers. Origen replies with a diatribe against the philosophers, who are all divided among themselves and are in disagreement on virtually every point. When he lists what he considers the pernicious errors of the philosophers, which can be healed only by the Christian Faith, he says *inter alia*: "And some have had to endure the mean-

[3] Gregory of Nyssa, *The Ascent of Moses*: PG 44, 337 AB; cf. J. Daniélou, "Metempsychosis in Gregory of Nyssa", in *Or. Chr. Per.* (1973), 227–43.

ingless doctrine of the transmigration of souls from
'doctors' who pull down rational nature sometimes to
utterly irrational nature [= the animals], sometimes to
nature without feeling [= plants]. If we are to bring
these persons healing, how could we do other than im-
prove the souls of those who have converted to the
Christian teaching? For this teaching does not prescribe
blunt stupidity or the loss of reason as punishment for
the wicked but rather shows that the sufferings and
punishments inflicted by God on the wicked are certain
medicines that are meant to bring about their conver-
sion." [4]

Reincarnation is a pagan madness from which one is
healed through the Christian Faith: this then is the view
of the famous Alexandrian master! He briefly adds one
of the arguments that one will find repeatedly in the
polemics against reincarnation: this doctrine makes the
idea of punishment an illusion and thus does harm to
morality.

Judaism could "flirt" with the idea of reincarnation.[5]
Why did Christianity never do so? We must now seek
the explanation of this, and since we cannot draw up a
complete dossier, we must concentrate on a few especially important texts from the first centuries of Christianity. It is only via these qualified witnesses that we

[4] Origen, *Contra Celsum* III, 75.
[5] Cf. G. Scholem, s.v. "Gilgul", in *Enc. Jud.* VII (1972), 573–77; M.
Gatser, s.v. "Transmigration (Jewish)", in *Encyclopaedia of Religion and
Ethics*, vol. XII (1921).

shall be able to grasp better the profound reasons for the Christian rejection of reincarnation.

We pass over the biblical texts, which are often made to serve as "evidence" that the idea of reincarnation was present in the teaching of Jesus and of earliest Christianity.[6] We shall find many of these texts again in our patristic texts.

a. *Gnosis and Reincarnation*

There were indeed Christians who taught reincarnation, but these were very controversial Christians: the gnostics. It is hard to get a clear view of the gnostic movement, not only because we lack sources (although the gnostic library discovered at Nag Hammadi has furnished us with a large quantity of new information), but above all because of its polymorphic and shifting syncretistic character. But we possess a good number of testimonies to the gnostics' idea of metempsychosis.[7] Gnosis is in a sense the fulcrum that allows us to study the Christian attitude to reincarnation. Gnosis is a radical new interpretation of Christianity, which does indeed make use of Christian material but alters its meaning radically. It is not possible to quote here the whole dossier of gnostic texts

---

[6] Cf. A. Orbe, *Textos y pasajes de la Escritura interesados en la teoría de la reincorporación*, in *Estudios Eclesiasticos* 33 (1959), 77–91.

[7] A very detailed overview is given by A. Orbe, *Cristología Gnóstica*, vol. II (Madrid, 1976) (B.A.C. vol. 385), 573–97.

that speak of reincarnation. I choose a few very typical texts, which allow us to see an initial outline of the Christian view, on the basis of which gnostic ideas were rejected.

Let us take as our first example the gnostic exposition of Matthew 5:25–26: "Make friends quickly with your accuser, while you are going with him to court, lest your accuser hand you over to the judge, and the judge to the guard, and you be put in prison: truly, I say to you, you will never get out till you have paid the last penny."

Irenaeus tells us that the gnostic Carpocrates and his school interpreted these verses as follows:

The accuser: this is one of the angels of the world, whom they call the devil, who was created in order to lead the lost souls out of the world to the prince (*Archōn*), the first of the angels who made the world. He hands over such souls to another angel, who serves him, so that he may enclose them in other bodies, for the body is a prison. And the words "you will never get out till you have paid the last penny" mean that he will not escape from the power of the angels who made the world. Rather, he will be transferred into other bodies until he has performed every deed that exists in the world; it is only when none of these is still lacking that the soul becomes free and available to that God who stands above the prince of the world. Thus, souls are redeemed and set free, either by having been active at the very beginning in all actions or else by discharging their

debt to the full by wandering from body to body and becoming immersed in every kind of life. Then they no
longer need to dwell in a body.[8]

There is nothing very surprising in the methodology
of this exegesis. The allegorical exegesis is wholly acceptable at this period. It is the contents that are surprising. The *Archōn* in the form of the judge in the Gospel
text is the evil creator of this evil world. The only way
to come out of the prisons of this world, i.e., out of the
bodies, is through a total liberation of the soul from this
world. This view of the world and of man determines
the choice of particular scriptural texts that are ex-
pounded in the sense of reincarnation. It is not the
scriptural text that is determinative for the view of
world and man; on the contrary, it is a prior understanding of these that determines the interpretation of
the sacred text. The reading of the texts, in keeping
with this, is fragmentary, breaking the texts up through
artificial incisions that pay no heed to the context.

Let us look at another example of such an exegesis.
Saint Paul says at Romans 7:9a: "I lived once without
the law." However, he himself observes in other places
that he never lived without the law, since he was a
born and circumcised Jew who had followed the Mosaic law since birth (cf. Phil 3:5; Gal 1:13–14). For Basi-

[8] Irenaeus of Lyons, *Adv. haer.*, 1, 25, 4. On the exegetical method of
the gnostics, cf. J.-M. Poffet, *La méthode exégétique d'Héracléon et
d'Origène, commentateurs de Jn 4: Jésus, la Samaritaine et les Samaritains* (Fribourg, Switzerland, 1985) (= Paradosis vol. 28).

lides, one of the chief figures of gnosticism, this text cannot mean anything other than that Saint Paul lived without the law in earlier existences. According to Origen, Basilides is supposed to have said: " 'I lived once without the law': that is to say, 'before I came into this body, I lived in a kind of body that is not subordinate to the law, for example in the body of an animal or a bird'." Origen cannot avoid calling this "crazy, godless fables".[9]

A third example will complete our selection: we read in Clement of Alexandria's *Excerpts from Theodotos*: "The adherents of Basilides assert that the text: 'God avenges sins unto the third and the fourth generation' (cf. Ex 34:7) refers to the 'reincarnations'."[10] For Basilides, it is clear that there were no other possible punishments for sins than the reincarnation of souls in a sequence of different bodies.[11]

It would be easy to make this list longer. It seems that the gnostics had assembled collections of scriptural testimonies that were designed to prove that Scripture teaches rebirth.[12] Saint Irenaeus accused such an exegesis of employing scriptural texts like the stones of a mosaic that have all been broken off from one and the

---

[9] Origen, *Ad Romanos* v, 1; PG 14, 1014 C – 1015 A and 1083 A; cf. A. Orbe's essay "S. Metodio y la exégesis de Rom 7, 9a: 'Ego autem vivebam sine lege aliquando' ", in *Gregorianum* 50 (1969), 93–139, at 105.

[10] *Excerpta ex Theodoto*, 28; SC 23, 119.

[11] Cf. Orbe, *Cristología Gnóstica*, 583f.

[12] Cf. Orbe, *Textos y pasajes*, 78 and 90.

same picture but are now being used to fabricate a quite different picture. The one who refuses to be deceived by this process will "indeed acknowledge the names and phrases and parables from the Scriptures, but not their blasphemous lunacies. He will indeed recognize the stones from the mosaic, but he will not take the fox to be an image of the king." [13]

Reincarnation, which the gnostics find attested in Scripture, is in reality an integral element of an anthropological and cosmological system that as such was incompatible with the "system" of biblical revelation, even if one or other text, taken in isolation, appeared to say the opposite. This becomes obvious when one sees how some gnostics interpret redemption as a liberation from the cycle of rebirths. We can see this in a text of Saint Irenaeus that is extremely illuminating for our subject:

> They [the Ophites] wish to prove that the Christ descended on Jesus and then ascended from him, by arguing that according to the testimony of the disciples, Jesus did not do anything great either before the baptism or after his Resurrection; for the disciples did not know that Jesus was united with Christ . . . , and held his psychic body to be a cosmic body. After his Resurrection, he remained for a further eighteen months, and, when knowledge descended on him, he learned what the truth is. But he communicated this only to those few of his disciples whom he knew to be capable of grasping such great mysteries. So he as-

[13] Irenaeus, *Adv. haer.* 1, 9, 4.

cended into heaven, where Christ was seated at the right
hand of his Father Ialdabaoth, in order to receive into himself the souls of those who had known him and Christ after
they have put off their cosmic flesh, and to enrich himself
thereby. But the Father does not perceive and see that, just
as Jesus enriches himself with the holy souls, he himself suffers the same amount of loss, since he loses some of his
own strength through the souls. Thus he will ultimately no
longer be capable of sending holy souls into the world, but
only those who share in his own essence, i.e., those who
are born of the inbreathing. . . . The perfection will come
when the entire dew of the light-spirit is gathered together
and borne over into the imperishable aeon.[14]

This text really requires a very detailed commentary;
let us simply refer to some important elements. Christ
and Jesus are not identical. At the baptism, Christ, a
heavenly being, the Son of the true God, descends on
Jesus, who was "more righteous, more pure, and more
wise than all men";[15] but when Jesus was about to be
crucified, "Christ crossed over from him into an imperishable aeon, but Jesus was crucified." [16] Through
this Christ, Jesus was raised up, but not (as the "simple-
minded Christians" think) "in his cosmic body"; for the
gnostics, this is "the greatest error". No, Jesus rose up
in what they call a "psychic, pneumatic body" that no
longer has anything in common with the "cosmic ele-

14 Ibid., I, 30, 14.
15 Ibid., I, 30, 12.
16 Ibid., I, 30, 13.

ments" that Jesus has left behind in this world.[17] "The precise truth" that Jesus discovered during the eighteen months he spent on earth after the Resurrection is the truth that his Father Ialdabaoth is not the true God but a lesser god who is jealous of the true God and prevents the knowledge of him. The Father of Jesus is no other than the God of the Old Covenant, the Creator of this world, who rules over it thanks to the cosmic powers whom the other gnostics call the Archontes. Before his Ascension, Jesus teaches the small number of his true disciples, the gnostics, the secret doctrine based on this higher gnosis (while the apostles and their successors have fallen into error!). He sits now at the *right hand* of his Father, and the Ophites teach that this means he is now *superior* to his Father, since the right hand denotes the superiority that consists in the gnosis received from the heavenly Christ.

One could be tempted to reach out for Freudian categories when one reads this account of the slow decline of the Father—this evil, jealous being—and the irresistible ascent of his Son, Jesus. It is not without reason that one branch of depth psychology (the school of C. G. Jung) has been so interested in the gnostic myths. Our theme is more directly interested in the idea of a progressive victory over the inexorable law of rebirth. In my view, we find clearly in this text evidence that for the gnostics reincarnation was bound to the govern-

[17] Ibid.

ment of the "god of this world", the demiurge, the
Creator of this world, which is chained to matter. It is
he who possesses the power to send the souls back into
this world.

For gnosis, there does exist an end of the cycle of rebirths, and this end is connected with the mission of
Christ. Christ is in fact the Redeemer. The gnostics
have no difficulty in saying this, and it was precisely this
that made gnosis so difficult to refute. Gnosis is a kind
of contamination of language in which the words, although apparently retaining their Christian meaning,
are emptied of their meaning and are employed to express the opposite of what they originally mean, but in
such a way that this perversion does not clearly emerge
to view.

Christ is the one who brings salvation. Salvation in
the gnostic sense, however, consists in nothing other
than in the disillusioned knowledge of the long sequence of errors in which the Old Testament consists.
The gnostic Christ brings salvation through the knowledge (gnosis) that he brings of the right path that leads
out of this wicked world; by finding this path, the true
gnostics are freed from the cycle of rebirths. Thus
Christ's Ascension takes on a great significance for salvation in the gnostic sense. Salvation consists in the
egress of the soul, the divine particle, from this sublu-
nary world into which it has sunk down and in which
the merciless law of *heimarmenê*, the inexorable destiny,
holds sway. Here, the pseudo-Christian gnosis depends

strongly on the doctrines about the soul that we already find in the Hermetic gnosis of *Poimandres* and other texts in the *Corpus Hermeticum*.[18] The Docetists of whom Hippolytus writes could teach: "The transmigration of souls ceased when the Redeemer came." [19] As we have seen (and as Hippolytus' text confirms),[20] their doctrine that such a *metensômatôsis* (wandering of the soul from body to body) exists and that it has been conquered by the Redeemer is linked to a view of the soul and of its salvation that has gone very far from the Christian view.

b. *Christian Anthropology in Contrast to Reincarnation*

We have been able to adduce only a small selection of gnostic texts that touch on our subject. The same is true of the very numerous Christian texts that discuss reincarnation. Our aim has not been to give exhaustive information, for, as a proverb quoted by Saint Irenaeus says, "One need not drink the whole of the sea in order to recognize that its water is salty." [21] We shall limit our

[18] Cf. A.-J. Festugière's great study *La Révélation d'Hermes Trismégiste*, vol. III: *Les doctrines de l'âme* (Paris, 1953).

[19] *Ref.* VIII, 10, 1–2; GCS ed. Wendland 229; PG 16, 3354 BC.

[20] According to him, the Docetists consider the God of Moses, i.e., the God who created the world, to be a perverse being who maintains in power a lordship of error. It is he who causes the *metensômatôsis* of the souls. The Redeemer, who conceals himself in a body, has come to make an end of this error—at least for those who possess the true gnosis (ibid.).

[21] *Adv. haer.* II, 19, 8.

investigation to a few main texts, emphasizing the specific and new elements that each text brings in relation to the others.

Irenaeus of Lyons: A Biblical Anthropology Gains Acceptance

Testimonies from the period prior to Irenaeus do exist,[22] but it is in him, at the end of the second century, that we find the first detailed exposition of the reasons why Christianity rejects the doctrines of the transmigration of souls that it encounters at this period.

The most detailed text of Saint Irenaeus on our problem is found in his refutation of the gnosis of Carpocrates. He begins by demonstrating the inconsistencies of Carpocrates' doctrine of *metensômatôsis*[23] and then goes on to set out positively the Christian teaching.

> Their doctrine of the transmigration of souls [*metensômatôsis*] is refuted by the fact that the souls no longer recall in any way that which previously existed. For if they were sent out in order to experience everything, then they would also have to be able to recall what lay in the past, in order to accomplish what was still lacking—otherwise, they would continually strive miserably to do exactly the same things. If this was the reason for their coming on

[22] Theophilus of Antioch, *Ad Autol.* III, 7: PG 6, 1132 A; SC 20, 219; Justin, *Dial.* IV, 6–7; PG 6, 485 BC; Hermias: PG 6, 1169–72.

[23] This is how Irenaeus, followed by most of the Church Fathers, speaks of reincarnation; cf. A. Rousseau in the explanatory note to *Adv. haer.* II, 33, 1: SC 293, 337f.

earth, then the fact of being united to the body would not be able to extinguish totally the recollection of the past and reflection upon it. For what the soul now sees in itself and experiences in a dream while the body sleeps, it imparts to the greater part of the body in keeping with its memory, and sometimes it happens that one relates in a waking state, a long time afterward, what he has seen in a dream. Thus the soul would also have to remember what it had done before entering the body. For if it knows even after the dream what it saw in a moment and received in the dream, after it has communicated itself once again to the body and has distributed itself among every member, then all the more ought it to know where it was for such a long time, and to know the entire eternity of its past life.[24]

This argumentation presupposes that even the adherents of reincarnation did not assert that they had "recollections of earlier lives on earth". This argument returns often both in the pagan and in the Christian polemic against the doctrine of reincarnation, and the alleged "recognitions" of Pythagoras, to which the Pythagoreans appealed in support of their master's doctrine of rebirth, were an easy target for the authors of comedies. In the much-discussed "reincarnationist" myth of Er the Pamphylian, Plato himself, at the end of the *Republic*, has the "drink of forgetting" intervene in order to explain the lack of exact memories of previous lives on earth.[25] In connection with our text, Irenaeus also

[24] *Adv. haer.* II, 33, 1.
[25] *Republic* x, 13–16; 614a–21d.

speaks of the Platonic myth and criticizes its anthropological inconsistency.[26] We cannot go into the individual details of Irenaeus' anthropology here, his theory of
sleep and dreams,[27] and the view he presupposes of the
connection between soul and body. Since the soul has
an activity of its own while the body sleeps, it can remember this activity when it reenters the body (so to
speak); all the more ought it then to retain the recollection of an earlier life, if such a life had existed.

Irenaeus does not limit himself only to this empirical
argument, however. Did he sense that such an argumentation on the basis of the lack of experiences from
earlier lives on earth threatens to be deprived of its
force by contrary experiences? This is in fact the question posed by numerous experiences today that can be
interpreted in the sense of reincarnation, whether we
take the cases studied by Dr. Stevenson or the thera-
peutic experiences presented by Denise Desjardins and
others.[28]

Let me recall here in a brief excursus what Aristotle
says at the beginning of his *Metaphysics*: *experience as such
does not yet explain anything.* "Experience", says Aristotle,
"knows only the fact [*to hoti*] but not the why [*di hoti*]."
This or that experience, taken by itself, proves nothing;

[26] *Adv. haer.* II, 33, 2–3.

[27] Cf. M. Spanneut, *Le stoïcisme des Pères de l'Eglise, de Clément de
Rome à Clément d'Alexandrie* (Paris, 1957), 217–18, 229.

[28] I. Stevenson, *Twenty Cases Suggestive of Reincarnation* (New York,
1966) (cf. n. 75 below); D. Desjardins, *La mémoire des vies antérieures*
(Paris, 1980).

it is only when one knows its "why", its cause, that one can assign it a place in a structured knowledge, in a science.[29] The structured knowledge to which Saint Irenaeus appeals in order to interpret the experiences is that of the Christian Faith, which is based on revelation. This process is not in the least unjustified. Every interpretation is made in the light of a knowledge that is not simply generated by an experience but precedes it and is the very basis of the possibility of understanding what one has experienced. This is true both for the adherents of reincarnation and for those who reject it. It is only in the light of a certain prior understanding that one will be able to interpret a particular experience as "recollection of an earlier life".[30]

For Irenaeus, the profound reason for the rejection of *metensômatôsis* lies in the very nature of man, who is understood in harmony with the doctrine of revelation as God's creature: "Each one of us has his own soul, just as he also receives his own body thanks to the divine ordering of things. For God is not so poor or so limited that he would not be able to give each one his own body, his own soul, and his own character" (*charaktêra*).[31]

---

[29] *Metaphysics* A, 1, 981ab.

[30] Denise Desjardins herself says this clearly, by showing that the doctrine of the earlier lives is an integral element of a world-view and an image of man in which "one individual element cannot be separated from the path as a whole" (*La mémoire*, 245). It is a methodological error to believe that one can empirically *demonstrate* the transmigration of souls through experiences and experiments.

[31] *Adv. haer.* II, 33, 5.

Man is neither a particle of God that has sunk down into the material world nor a preliminary manifestation of the absolute. He is a creature! This is the new light that revelation sheds on man, on his nature and his experiences. He is a creature, i.e., willed by God, and willed as such with *this* body and *this* soul, and hence in his inalienable identity.[32] If man is created by God and consequently is willed as such, then this holds true of all men. Irenaeus deduces from this the following conclusion against the idea of reincarnation:

> When therefore the number that he himself has preordained by himself is full, then all who are inscribed (in the book of life) will arise to life and will have their own bodies, their own souls, and their own spirit[33] in which they pleased God. But those who deserve punishment will also be subjected to this and will likewise have their souls and their bodies in which they displeased God. Then neither the one group nor the other will beget nor be begotten, will take either wife or husband (cf. Mt 22:30), so that what the Father has ordained may be fulfilled through the completing of the mutually corresponding number that God has preordained.[34]

[32] I have set out elsewhere the consequences of this faith: "L'homme créé par Dieu: le fondement de la dignité de l'homme", in *Gregorianum* 65 (1984), 337–63.

[33] This "trichotomy" (body, soul, spirit) is typical of the anthropology of Irenaeus. A perfect man is one who has received anew the Holy Spirit who was lost through the fall; cf. A. Rousseau's commentary in SC 193, 339–42.

[34] *Adv. haer.*, II, 33, 5.

Thus, Irenaeus can infer from faith in one Creator God the uniqueness of the life of each man and the uniqueness of mankind as a whole. Thus he excludes every cyclic view. Man has a unique history before God, for God has created him and willed him in his uniqueness. A unique life thereby becomes the place where the definitive destiny of man is decided, and each man will enter eternal life in terms of soul and body in this personal uniqueness. Mankind as a whole has likewise a unique history, which began through God's creative act in freedom and will be brought to completion in freedom by the same Creator.

The Christian faith in the inalienable uniqueness of every man did however encounter a difficulty that was often raised in antiquity: If Christian faith holds that the human soul has been created, how can it simultaneously maintain that the soul is immortal? Irenaeus pertinently summarizes the arguments of the pagan philosophers. "It is impossible that souls, whose existence began only a short time before, should continue to exist for a long time; if they are immortal, then they must also be unbegotten, but if they have had a beginning through an act of begetting, then they must die along with the body." [35] Faith in creation indicates the way out of this dilemma: God alone is "without beginning and end"; "but everything that has been made by him . . . has its beginning in its coming into being." God gives it be-

[35] Ibid., 34, 2.

coming and being, so that "everything had once a beginning in its existence and continues for as long as
God wills its existence and continuation." [36]

It is not so much because of this or that individual
point that Saint Irenaeus rejects reincarnation; *the Christian Faith in its totality resists this view*. The fact that man
is created with *this* soul and *this* body; that this spiritual
soul has a beginning but receives an indestructible life;
that this body is destined to resurrection and thereby to
eternal life; that man is summoned to give an answer
once and for all to the call of the Creator—all these are
integral elements of this view of man that the Christian
accepts as the revelation of the definitive truth. This vision cannot integrate into itself belief in reincarnation
without changing its very essence.

But what about Origen? One can often hear this
objection. After Irenaeus, this clear witness to the apostolic tradition in the ancient Church, we must accordingly turn to Origen, in order to see whether a
Christian doctrine of reincarnation does not exist at
least in him.

Origen: A Christian Who Teaches Reincarnation?

One cannot begin to treat of our subject without en-
countering the name of the great Alexandrian master.

[36] Ibid., 34, 2–3. This simple and illuminating answer also shows in
my view the solution to the much-disputed problem in theology of the
alleged antithesis between immortality of the soul and resurrection.

Origen is a mighty spirit, without doubt the most striking figure in Christian thought at the end of the period
of persecution. His work was immense, his influence
equally so. The condemnation of some of his doctrines
by the Fifth Ecumenical Council of Constantinople in
553, but the earlier hostility of Saint Jerome and others
had led to the loss of most of his works; yet even the
little that remains to us is very much.[37]

Did Origen teach *metensômatôsis*, reincarnation? Many
assert this, from Saint Jerome onward. And yet Origen
rejects this doctrine as explicitly as possible. Did he perhaps teach it in an esoteric instruction, although he rejected it in his public teaching? In my view, the
question, despite its difficulties, is ultimately very simple. Origen taught the preexistence of souls and their
incarnation in bodies, but not their reincarnation. Let
us look more closely at this.

In his commentary on the Gospel of John, Origen
draws up the program of the questions that a tractate on
the soul (which he wanted to write, but finally never
composed) would have to analyze:[38]

> One must study in another place, more carefully and
> deeply, and taken by themselves, the questions of the es-
> sence of the soul, of the origin of its existence, of its entry

[37] For more details, cf. the great work of P. Nautin, *Origène. Sa vie et
son oeuvre* (Paris, 1977), and H. Crouzel's *Bibliographie critique d'Origène*
(Hague, 1971).

[38] Cf. Pamphilius, *Apol. pro Orig.*, chap. VIII: PG 17, 603 C – 604 A.

into this earthly body, of the elements making up the life of each soul, and of its liberation from here below. One must see whether or not it is possible that it enters a body for a second time, whether this is in accordance with the same cycle and the same ordinance or not, in the same body or in another; and if in the same body, whether this remains substantially identical with itself although it takes on other properties, or whether it remains the same in terms of substance *and* of properties, and whether the soul always makes use of the same body, or changes bodies. Here one must investigate what reincarnation really is and how it is different from incarnation, and whether the one who maintains the reality of reincarnation consequently holds that the world is imperishable. It will also be necessary to present in this connection the theories of those who assert that, according to Scripture, the soul enters the body with the sperm, and the consequences resulting from this.

To sum up: since the theory about the soul is wide and difficult and must be deepened on the basis of the sporadic indications of Scripture, it requires a specific study.[39]

Origen thus invites us to keep initially and above all, in this "wide and difficult" question, to the indications that Scripture gives us, although these are only "sporadic". Let us therefore see how Origen discusses the texts that can be interpreted in the sense of reincarnation, and let us then study the difficult problem of what Origen himself teaches.

[39] *In Joannem* VI, 14 nos. 85–87; cf. A.-J. Festugière, *La Révélation*, 14.

Many scriptural passages have been, and still are, interpreted as "biblical proofs" of reincarnation. One of the most celebrated is surely that concerning the identity between the prophet Elijah and John the Baptist. Let us see how Origen expounds this passage in his commentaries on the Gospels of John and Matthew.

When the scribes ask John "Are you Elijah?", he replies, "I am not" (Jn 1:21). And yet this same John is announced as the Elijah who is to return (cf. Lk 1:11, 17):

> As for the first quotation, one will say that John did not know that he was Elijah, and those who see in this an argument for reincarnation will perhaps make use of this in the theory that the soul takes on a sequence of bodies and does not retain any recollection of the earlier existences. The same people will assert that some Jews, because they held this view, said of the Redeemer that he was one of the ancient prophets (cf. Lk 9:19)—not arisen from the grave but born again. For if they were certain of their facts when they called Mary his mother and held the carpenter Joseph to be his father (cf. Mk 6:3), how then could they believe that he was one of the prophets risen from the dead (cf. Lk 9:8)? By employing the passage Genesis 7:4 (LXX), "I will eradicate every resurrection", the same interpreters will bring into perplexity the one who is concerned to refute all the deceitful arguments that can be drawn out of Scripture, and to remain true to the dogma.[40]

[40] Ibid., VI, 10, nos. 64f.

Origen contrasts this exegesis to that of the *ekklêsiasti-kos*, the "man of the Church", of whom he often speaks.[41] For him, this is not one who blindly holds fast to doctrines he does not understand but one who knows how to read Scripture in the place that is genuinely Scripture's own, namely, the Church:

> Another man, a member of the Church who rejects the doctrine of reincarnation as something that leads astray and does not admit that the soul of John was ever Elijah, will have recourse to the already-mentioned words of the angel who spoke, in reference to the birth of John, not of the *soul* of Elijah but of his spirit and his power, as follows: "He will go before the Lord with the spirit and the power of Elijah, to turn the hearts of the fathers back to the children" (Lk 1:17), for he will be able to prove by means of thousands of examples from the Scriptures that the spirit is something other than the soul and that what one calls "power" is something other than the spirit and the soul. But this is not the right moment to quote a great number of such texts, for that would lengthen our exposition greatly. In favor of the distinction between "power" and "spirit", the following text will suffice for the present: "The Holy Spirit will come over you, and the power of the Most High will overshadow you" (Lk 1:35), and these other texts that show that the spirits in the prophets have been given them by God and yet are called their own pos-

[41] Cf. H. de Lubac, *Geist aus der Geschichte. Das Schriftverständnis von Origenes* (Einsiedeln, 1968), above all the chapter "Origenes als Mann der Kirche".

session: "The spirits of the prophets are subject to the prophets" (1 Cor 14:2) and "The spirit of Elijah descended on Elisha" (2 Kings 2:15). Thus he will say that it is not in the least surprising that John, who turns the hearts of the fathers back to the children with the spirit and the power of Elijah, is called Elijah who is to return, on the basis of this spirit. In order to demonstrate this, he will make use of the following argument: if the God of the universe unites himself very deeply to the saints and becomes their God, and for this reason is called the God of Abraham, the God of Isaac, and the God of Jacob, how then *a fortiori* will not the Holy Spirit, who is united to the prophets, be able to be called their Spirit, so that the Spirit is called the Spirit of Elijah and the Spirit of Isaiah! [42]

Elijah—so mysterious and such an important figure in the Jewish tradition[43]—cannot serve as an argument in favor of reincarnation, as Origen goes on to explain, for Elijah is not dead: rather, he was taken up alive from this earth. His return could not be a new embodiment of his soul in another body, but only the return of the body that was taken up.[44]

In his commentary on Matthew, Origen speaks of reincarnation when commenting on two other texts that are often brought forward as a testimony to this doctrine. In Matthew 14:1–2, Herod says of Jesus: "This is

[42] *In Joannem* VI, 9, nos. 66–68.

[43] Cf. J. Stiassny, "Elie dans le judaïsme", in *Etudes carmélitaines*, vol. 25, 2 (Paris, 1956).

[44] *In Joannem* VI, 9, nos. 70–71.

John the Baptist." In the view of some people, Herod
believed in reincarnation. This *pseudodoxia*, as Origen
calls it, is incorrect, for John the Baptist was born a
mere six months before Jesus. According to Origen, the
meaning of this passage is rather that Herod believed
that it was a question of one and the same person, of
John, "who has been raised from the dead after he had
been beheaded, and was [now] called Jesus".[45]

The passage about the little dogs under the table, in
the narrative of Jesus' encounter with the Canaanite
woman (Mt 15:21–25), offers an apparent reason to find
reincarnation in the Bible: these little dogs would be
souls that had crossed over into the bodies of animals.
Origen gives a clear answer to this:

> Others who are alien to the ecclesiastical teaching wish to
> express the view that the souls have wandered out of
> human bodies, in keeping with their varied wickedness,
> into the bodies of dogs. *But we have not at all found this in
> Sacred Scripture*; therefore we say that the more rational dis-
> position has turned into a more irrational disposition, suf-
> fering this because of much carelessness and negligence. In
> a similar manner, a free will too, which has become less
> rational through neglecting the matters of reason, some-
> times turns around and becomes rational, so that the for-
> mer little dog that loves to eat *of the crumbs that fall from the
> table of its masters* arrives at the condition of being a child.
> For virtue contributes much to making someone a child of
> God. But wickedness and lack of self-control in arrogant

[45] *In Matth.* x, 20.

speech and shamelessness lead to his being called (in Scripture's phrase) a dog. You are to think along these lines in the case of the other names that suit the irrational beasts.[46]

The *ekklêsiastikos logos*, the instruction of the Church, does not know this teaching: it is a dogma foreign to the Church of God.[47] How then was it possible to accuse an author who so decidedly takes up a position hostile to the doctrine of reincarnation of teaching the opposite? It is difficult to reconstruct the facts of the case. Some enemies of Origen assert that this doctrine is found in his work *Peri Archōn*, which we have only in the Latin translation made by Rufinus, an admirer and defender of Origen. Did he perhaps leave out the passages that had been attacked in order to salvage the orthodoxy of their author? Saint Jerome, who does not exactly spare the memory of Origen, quotes from passages that one does not find in Rufinus' translation. The passage that is closest to a doctrine of reincarnation is however reproduced by Jerome only in a summary. Jerome's text is as follows:

In order to conclude [his presentation of the creatures endowed with responsibility, Origen] discussed in great detail the following point: an angel, a soul, or at least a

[46] Ibid., xi, 17. H. de Lubac has followed up the history of this *topos* of the man who changes into an animal because of his vices in *Pic de la Mirandole* (Paris, 1974), 184–93; cf. also H. Crouzel, *Théologie de l'image de Dieu chez Origène* (Paris, 1956), 220–305.

[47] *In Matth.* xiii, according to Pamphilius, *Apol. pro Orig.*, chap. x: PG 17, 612 A.

demon—he says of these that they have the same nature
but different inclinations—can become a beast of burden
in keeping with the measure of their negligence, and after
they have suffered tortures and the heat of fire, they can
choose whether to become an irrational animal and dwell
in the waters or waves or to take on the body of this or
that animal, so that we must fear, not only the bodies of
the quadrupeds, but also those of the fishes.[48]

Even if this text were to reproduce exactly the thinking of Origen, the question remains: Is he speaking of
reincarnation? Pamphilius, who tells us that Origen was
accused of teaching reincarnation, says that Origen is
speaking here not of reincarnation but of the souls of
animals.[49] Thus, this text would be discussing the origin
of the animal's soul. Jerome, who is enraged at "this
disgusting treatise, through which he [Origen] has
wounded the soul of his reader", must however con-
cede that Origen's aim is "to escape the charge that he
professes *metempsychôsis*, which belongs to the doctrine
of Pythagoras".[50] Other texts, however, provide Jerome
with the clear proof that Origen taught Pythagoras' and
Plato's doctrine of the transmigration of souls.[51] But
when one looks more closely at them, these passages
talk about something else. What Jerome represents as

[48] *Ep.* 124, 4; cf. the commentary on this passage by H. Crouzel and
M. Simonetti in Origen, *Traité des principes*, vol. II: SC 253, 119–25.

[49] *Apol. pro Orig.*, chap. IX: PG 17, 608 A.

[50] *Ep.* CXXIV, 4.

[51] Ibid., VII, 10, 14.

metempsychôsis is in reality, as Origen himself says, the *ensômatôsis* of souls.[52] Origen seeks to respond through his theory of the preexistence of souls and their "embodiment" to a weighty objection to belief in a Creator God: Why are men born unequal, some as free men and others as slaves, some talented and some not, some in a rich family or a cultivated people, others in misery or in barbarism? If one extends the question to all the spiritual natures, one could add: "Why are some beings heavenly and others human, and why does there exist a hierarchy among the angels themselves?"[53] The doctrine of reincarnation is proposed as an answer to these questions, but Origen's theory attempts to give a different answer. According to him, God created all souls equal in rank and similar. The cause of the inequality lies not in any injustice on the part of the Creator but in the freedom of the souls. They receive the rank that corresponds to them in keeping with their virtue or negligence: this rank can go from that of the highest angels to that of the "sea monsters". Does Origen think that the animals are incarnations of souls that have fallen so deeply? It seems that the problem with which Origen is concerned in these contested passages is rather the problem of the devil, the fallen angel, who is linked with the "sea monsters that are mentioned in various

[52] The two concepts are explicitly distinguished from one another in *In Joannem* VI, 14, no. 86.

[53] P. Nautin, *Origène*, 123, on *De princ.* I, 8, 2.

passages of the Bible and are traditionally understood as an incarnation of the devil".[54]

Origen expresses all this as a supposition, not so much as a developed philosophical system, and it also happens that he "very explicitly rejects this idea of a 'fall of the soul as far as into the animals' ".[55] He seems also to have envisaged hypothetically the possibility that souls, after once returning to the original unity, could experience a new embodiment (*ensômatôsis*) in a new world cycle. This hypothesis would lie behind some texts to which Jerome takes exception. But here too there would be no reincarnation: "His hypothesis included one single incarnation of the soul in each world." [56]

Origen was an intellect far too powerful to be capable of reduction to a system. In the difficult question of the creation of the soul, he decided in favor of a view that the Church subsequently rejected: the idea of the preexistence of the soul. It was *this* teaching that the Council of 553 condemned. Since many of Origen's writings perished as a consequence of this condemnation, it is difficult to make a precise estimate of his thinking, all the more so because this is a thinking in the process of seeking: one must not forget that Origen was a pioneer in many ways. But if one must make a

54 Ibid., 124.
55 Ibid., 125, on *Contra Celsum* VIII, 30.
56 Ibid., 126.

brief answer to the question we posed at the beginning: "Is Origen the Christian teacher of reincarnation?" we must answer in the negative. And we can say still more. If Jerome can employ the accusation that Origen teaches *metempsychôsis*, in order to blacken his name, this proves clearly how unacceptable this doctrine was for Christians, for Jerome could not have leveled this charge if the doctrine of reincarnation had been compatible with the Christian Faith. We can add a further argument on the same lines: it appears that Origen himself reacted so violently against the *pseudodoxia* of reincarnation because he wanted to aver his own orthodoxy. Would he have done so if this doctrine had been more or less tolerated in Christianity? [57]

Origen is thus not the Christian teacher of reincarnation, but is doubtless the early Christian author who can most easily be understood in this sense. His hypotheses about eschatology and about the "fluctuations" through which souls can pass ("Even if they are raised up to heaven in the course of one aeon, they can become lame in the course of the following aeon, and can become demons")[58] have repeatedly aroused the suspicion that Origen was a reincarnationist. In his irresolution, however, he did find a firm standpoint: Origen believed

---

[57] Cf. H. J. Vogt's note in *Origenes. Der Kommentar zum Evangelium nach Matthäus*, vol. 1 (Stuttgart, 1983) (= Bibliothek der griechischen Literatur, vol. 18), 280.

[58] This is how P. Nemeshegyi summarizes Origen's hypothesis in *La paternité de Dieu chez Origène* (Paris and Tournai, 1960), 218.

with all his heart that "love never ceases" (1 Cor 13:8),
and it was in love that he found the answer to his great
question, which is the nodal point of all his hypotheses:
How can human freedom, created freedom, escape the
alteration and the instability that we all experience pain-
fully and find a definitive stability in that which is
good? Origen says in a commentary on the Letter to
the Romans:

> The Apostle teaches us in a short sentence what it is that
> would retain free will in the future times, so that it does
> not fall back into sin, when he says: "Love never ceases"
> (1 Cor 13:8). It is said here that love is greater than faith
> and hope, because it is only through love that one will be
> henceforth incapable of committing sin. If the soul attains
> to such a level of perfection that it loves God with all its
> heart, all its soul, and all its force, and loves its neighbor as
> itself, where would there then be any place for sin? [59]

We have not in the least given an exhaustive treat-
ment of the patristic dossier on reincarnation with this
brief presentation of the positions of Irenaeus and Origen. Let it suffice here to recall briefly the chief actors
whom we should have to study if our overview were to
be a little more complete.[60]

---

[59] *In Rom.* v, 10: PG 14, 1053 BC. P. Nemeshegyi also shows that this
text, which is not present in Rufinus' translation, faithfully presents Origen's thought (*La paternité*, 223).

[60] L. Bukowski, "La Réincarnation selon les Pères de l'Eglise", *Gregorianum* 9 (1928), 68–85, assembles a large number of texts; cf. also the
texts mentioned above (n. 22); cf. also the richly documented study by L.

First, we should have to study *Tertullian*. In his treatise *De Anima* (composed between 210 and 213), he devotes a long excursus to the question of *metempsychôsis*. He begins by attacking the alleged reincarnations of Pythagoras and goes on to refute Plato, opposing the linear view of salvation history to the idea of a cyclic time. He then discusses the teaching of Empedocles on the reincarnations in animals and finally criticizes the gnostic theories and their exegesis.[61] Unlike Origen, Tertullian teaches the simultaneous origin of the soul and the body, which gives him occasion to teach "traducianism". His aim is quite clearly to oppose faith in the Resurrection to the idea of reincarnation (*fiducia christianorum resurrectio mortuorum*—"the hope of Christians is the resurrection of the dead").[62] The Resurrection of Christ is the hinge of this hope: the identity of the glorified body of the risen Christ with his earthly body is the strongest barrier set up against the *metempsychôsis*.[63]

We should then have to study *Lactantius*, whose anthropology is structured wholly in harmony with the Christian premises. If one believes in a God who has

---

Scheffczyk, "Der Reinkarnationsgedanke in der altchristlichen Literatur", *Sitzungsberichte der Bayerischen Akademie der Wissenschaften, philos.-histor. Kl.*, 1985, fasc. 4 (Munich, 1985), bibliography.

[61] *De anima* 28–35; cf. the notes in J. H. Waszink's critical edition (Amsterdam, 1947), 353–419.

[62] *De resurrectione carnis*, chap. 1: PL 2, 841 A.

[63] Cf. *De carne Christi*, chap. 24: PL 2, 836 BD.

created souls and bodies, reincarnation becomes meaningless: "It is not necessary for the old souls to put on
new bodies, since the same artist [God] who made the
first can also keep on making new ones." [64] One would
also have to mention *Gregory Nazianzen*,[65] *Gregory of
Nyssa*,[66] *Nemesius of Emesa*,[67] and many others.[68] But
above all, one would have to study in depth the lumi-
nous texts that Augustine dedicated to our theme or,
more generally, to the question of a cyclic view of
time.[69]

Henri-Charles Peuch summarizes as follows the
teaching of *Saint Augustine*: "Augustine opposes to the
philosophers' periods of time the *falsi circuli* or *falsus cir-
culus*, the *rectum iter*, the *recta via*, namely, Christ; to the
hellenistic repetition he opposes the Christian *novitas*; to
the perplexity of the pagans, who turn in circles, he opposes the bliss of the Christians, for whom the circle has
been broken thanks to the Lord. The whole finds its
summit in the statement of the First Letter of Peter:

---

[64] *Institutiones* 3, 19, 19; cf. M. Perrin, *L'homme antique et chrétien.
L'anthropologie de Lactance (*250 + 325)* (Paris, 1981), 324–27.

[65] Cf. *Or.* XXVII, 10 (Theol. I, 10) and n. 7 on p. 95 of SC 250.

[66] Cf. *Vita Moysis* (PG 44, 336f.), *De creat. hominis* (PG 44, 232 A – 233
B); *De anima et resurrectione* 14, 2–8 (PG 46, 108 B – 113 A); cf. also Daniélou,
"Metempsychosis".

[67] *De natura hominis* 2: PG 40, 577 B.

[68] Cf. Bukowski, "La Réincarnation", and the dossier drawn up long
ago by Fr. Baltus, S.J.: *Défense des SS. Pères accusés de Platonisme* (Paris,
1711), 290–310.

[69] *De civitate Dei* X, 30 and XII, 10–20.

Semel enim Christus mortuus est pro peccatis nostris." [70] The Christian view of time is based on the conviction that Christ has died for our sins once and for all (1 Pet 3:18); that he has risen from the dead, no more to die; that death has no more power over him (Rom 6:9) and that Christians are called to be always with the Lord after their resurrection (1 Th 4:17).[71] Thus everything forms one single history because there is only one single Christ event.

Saint Augustine summarizes here the entire tradition of early Christianity. The rejection of reincarnation has its ultimate roots in the Christian Faith itself, in its center, Christ, who is the midpoint and goal of history and in whom all the seeking of men comes to rest. And here too this seeking finds the answer to the fundamental question that motivates again and again the reincarnationist views: "How is it possible that an unhappy human life, in all its meaninglessness, in its blindnesses and its misery, all at once flows into eternity? How is it possible that an eternal reward, an eternal and unchangeable goal is set fast for us thanks to the good or evil movements of a free will that is so weak and eccentric, so sleepy as our will?" Christian faith gives the answer: "The dispropor-

[70] "La gnose et le temps", in *Eranos–Jahrbuck*, vol. xx (1951), 723; cf. also H.-J. Marrou, *L'ambivalence du temps de l'histoire chez saint Augustin* (Montreal and Paris, 1950); C. Journet, *L'Eglise du Verbe Incarné*, vol. III (Desclée de Brouwer, 1969), 43–59; S. Jaki, *Science and Creation: From Eternal Cycles to an Oscillating Universe* (Edinburgh: Scottish Academic Press, 1974), on Augustine, 177–83.

[71] Cf. *De civ. Dei* xii, 13, 2.

tion between the uncertainty of the journey and the importance of the goal is more than compensated for in reality, in an abundantly rich manner, by the generosity and love for mankind of our savior God." [72]

2. Reincarnation Today: The Answer of Faith

At the Fourth World Congress for Natural Medicine, held at Geneva in 1980, Dr. Nowrocki, psychotherapist at the University of Frankfurt, presented his experiences with patients whom he had "led back" to the moment of their birth; indeed, he lets them reexperience their time in the womb, the moment of their conception, and even the death that separated them from their earlier life, many deaths, many births, many earlier lives.[73] One can read in Denise Desjardins how such experiments are carried out and how psychic traumas appear to find their explanation and even their resolution along the path of such "leadings back".[74] More and more therapists employ this method. Are we heading toward a "scientific" proof of reincarnation? Some people[75]

---

[72] J. Maritain, "L'immortalité du soi", in *De Bergson à Thomas d'Aquin* (New York, 1944), 143 and 145.

[73] "Journal de Genève", June 2, 1980, p. 13.

[74] *La mémoire des vies antérieures* (Paris, 1980).

[75] Thus the famous and very cautious book by Dr. Ian Stevenson, *Twenty Cases Suggestive of Reincarnation*. Characteristically, the title of the German translation changes the "suggestive" into "proofs": *Reinkarnation. Der Mensch im Wandel von Tod und Wiedergeburt. 20 überzeugende und wissenschaftlich bewiesene Fälle* (Freiburg, 1976).

assert this, relying on experiences that "allow us to suppose the presence of repeated lives on earth".[76] The adjective *scientific*, which this literature is quick to employ, lends the accounts credit *a priori*, but there is insufficient examination of whether one can truly speak of "scientific proofs" in such cases.

Let us take as an example the celebrated "case of Bridey Murphy". An American, Ruth Simmons, reveals in a state of hypnosis many factors from an earlier life that she spent in the nineteenth century in Ireland under the name of Bridey Murphy. Investigations carried out at the relevant places show that numerous individual details, which Mrs. Simmons could not know in her present life, are correct.[77] Even if we presuppose that the investigations were not manipulated, one must however make a methodological observation: even if the facts of the matter prove to be correct, their interpretation remains subjective. One must distinguish between the circumstances of the experience and their interpretation. This distinction is often forgotten in the discussion of the "earlier lives". Naturally, it is not a question of denying genuine experiences. If a person asserts that she sees herself in a scenery of the nineteenth century, if she is able to give a detailed descrip-

[76] I mention two further examples from this large body of literature: Joan Grant and D. Kelsey, *Nos vies antérieures* (Paris, 1978); M. Bernstein, *Protokoll einer Wiedergeburt. Der Bericht über die wissenschaftlich untersuchtde Rückführung in ein früheres Leben* (Berne, 1973) (translated from English).

[77] Cf. Bernstein, *Protokoll.*

tion of a particular place and a particular landscape, and it is shown that these descriptions are correct, then one can only note these events with scrupulous care. But one moves onto another level when one attempts to interpret them.

As we have noted above, it is not sufficient simply to register accounts of experiences, if one wishes to formulate an explanatory theory. The experiences must be given a place in a broader framework. But an explanatory theory is never simply the outcome of the greatest possible number of experiential data. Rather, one must confront the data with general principles that themselves do not derive from experience but precede and illuminate it. The doctrine of reincarnation is such an explanatory theory, presupposing general principles in the light of which one interprets certain experiences. In this sense, there can never at any time exist a strictly scientific proof of reincarnation—or of the nonexistence of reincarnation. The theory of reincarnation is derived in reality from a philosophical or religious prior understanding of the nature of man, of his origin, and of the destiny determined for him. If one shares this view of man, one will interpret particular experiences as "proofs" of one's convictions. If one does not share it, one will derive other explanations from these experiences. The "case of Bridey Murphy", for example, could be interpreted as a parapsychical phenomenon. People at earlier periods would perhaps have thought of a "private revelation" or of the working of demons.

a. *Every Fourth European Believes in Reincarnation*

If then there exist no scientific proofs for or against re-incarnation, must we content ourselves with purely subjective or even arbitrary judgments? Certainly not. There do exist arguments *pro* and *contra*, but these lie on the philosophical or theological level. The argumentation that I propose is primarily theological. But before we speak of the theological reasons for the rejection of reincarnation by the Christian Faith, we must point out some historical connections.

According to a survey of the Gallup's American Institute of Public Opinion,[78] roughly one European in four believes in reincarnation. How are we to explain this success of a theory that is so alien to the Christian tradition? One cannot provide any "monocausal" explanation of this, but let us indicate one significant point. It is in the period of the Enlightenment that reincarnationist views arise in modern Europe. Gotthold Ephraim Lessing published in 1780 his famous work *Die Erziehung des Menschengeschlechts*. Full of optimism, he sees the history of mankind as an irresistible ascent to the light of the spirit. In the last sections, he expresses the hypothesis that this ascent could take place in a succession of ever more spiritualized lives on earth. This idea conquers others: Goethe and the Romantics take it

[78] Cf. J. Stoetzel, *Les valeurs du temps présent: une enquête* (Paris: PUF, 1983).

up anew.[79] Darwin's theory of evolution strengthens in many people the conviction of universal progress. Allan Kardec (1804–69), one of the great propagandists of spiritualism and the idea of reincarnation, had the following significant words inscribed on his tombstone in Paris: "To be born, to die, to be reborn, and to make continual progress: that is the law." [80]

This "Westernized" view of reincarnation is obviously very different from that of the Eastern religions, with their cyclic view of time, which is unacquainted with the idea of a universal progress. Reincarnation as the path of mankind's onward progress? This idea could develop only in the soil of the Christian culture of the West, with its concept of a "salvation history" that makes its way toward the kingdom of God. This means that the idea of reincarnation has itself undergone a profound change. For the religions of the East, reincarnation was and is a situation of wretchedness, which one must try to escape if possible: but in the West, under the influence of the idea of progress, it becomes indeed a kind of path of salvation. While the East sees the wheel of rebirth as a situation of painful bondage, reincarnation becomes in the West the path of progressive self-realization.

[79] Cf. E. Bock, *Wiederholte Erdenleben. Die Wiederverkörperungsidee in der deutschen Geistesgeschichte* (Stuttgart, 1967) (very well documented and written from an anthroposophist standpoint).

[80] Quoted from B. Kloppenburg, *La reencarnación* (Bogotà, 1979), 11. This book gives a good overview of the great success of the reincarnationist views in Latin America.

Why has Christianity always rejected the idea of reincarnation? As far as I know, the Church has never formally condemned the doctrine of reincarnation: not because she might regard it as a doctrine that could be compatible with the Christian faith, but on the contrary because reincarnation so obviously contradicts the very principles of this faith that a condemnation has never seemed necessary.[81] But which principles are these? Let us now conclude by setting them out briefly.

b. *"But Christ Is the End" (Hölderlin)*

For Christianity, man is a *creature*. This means first that he is willed by God in his entire reality, in his soul but also in his body. The body is not the prison of the soul but is likewise created. Indeed, it is destined for an eternal life through the "resurrection of the flesh"—an idea that is totally alien to the hellenistic world. Saint Paul provoked shouts of laughter when he began to speak of this on the Areopagus (Acts 17:32). If man—with body and soul—is a creature, then this means that he is willed by God as this particular man, as a person, with a unique origin and a unique life that is destined to be fulfilled in eternal life. Judaism too believes all this (at least in its dominant tradition).

---

[81] The Second Vatican Council speaks in *Lumen gentium*, no. 48, in order to reject the idea of reincarnation, of "the single course of our earthly life".

Christianity has an additional element that is decisive. In my view, it is above all this specific element that forbids it to make any compromise with the reincarnationistic teachings: Jesus Christ himself. The Christian Faith looks on him as the incarnate God, as the Word of God become flesh. But he has arisen in this flesh and has ascended to heaven, where he sits "at the right hand of the Father" in this flesh, and he will "come again in glory" in this eternally living, glorified flesh. Thus one understands that the whole hope of Christianity is directed to a goal that is like that of its Founder. One cannot picture this ultimate destiny as a return into other bodies and other lives on earth. This life here is already fellowship with Christ, a fellowship that unites in one "single body" the adherents of this path and makes them "members of Christ"; and when this life ends, there is no other destiny for the one who has lived in fellowship with the body of Christ than the full unfolding of this fellowship in the "resurrection of the flesh".

This, sketched in a few words, is the *fundamental experience of Christianity*. Reincarnation is not rejected for the sake of some abstract doctrines or because of a diehard holding fast to traditional dogmas. The fact that the Christian Faith has no place for the doctrine of reincarnation is a direct consequence of this fundamental experience, which Paul recapitulates in the famous sentence, "For me, life is Christ and death a gain" (Phil 1:21). *Life is Christ*. To die means to live in the truest sense, to live with Christ, to live as he lives: in this glorified flesh that he received from the Virgin Mary through the working of the Holy Spirit, in which he "sits at the right hand of the Father", in which he will come again in glory.

Reincarnation has no place in Christianity because *life in Christ* is already its ultimate goal. "But Christ is the end", says Hölderlin in the late hymn *Der Einzige*. What more could one seek, when one has found *him*? Have we not found *everything* in him? In him there is no place for the endless search, from life to life, for a distant, unattainable goal, for a perfection that is not to be reached in aeons. The end has come to us; it is already present (cf. 1 Cor 10:11). Man's long search is at an end. What we could not find through endless re-births has been given to us. "For we did not *seek*: we were *sought*." [82] God has found man: "For it was not the sheep that sought the shepherd, or the drachma the housewife (Lk 15:4–9). He himself bent down to earth and found his image; he himself went into the place where the sheep had wandered astray. He lifted it up *and put an end to the wandering*." [83]

After this return home, there is no more wandering. Will the father send the prodigal son away, now that he has returned home? And how could there be a "tomor-row" after the words "Today you will be with me in

---

[82] Nicolas Cabasilas, *Das Buch vom Leben in Christus*, trans. G. Hoch, 2nd ed. (Einsiedeln, 1981), 23 (= Christliche Meister, vol. 14).

[83] Ibid.

paradise", spoken to the robber on his right side by the Lord when he is raised up on the Cross—a "tomorrow" that would lead him back into a foreign place? The same Jesus said: "When I am lifted up from the earth, I shall draw all men to myself" (Jn 12:32), and: "I shall certainly not turn away the one who comes to me" (Jn 6:37). After this great reunion there is nothing more to be sought, for what we find here infinitely surpasses all that we had sought and waited for (cf. 1 Cor 2:9).[84]

[84] G. Adler, *Wiedergeboren nach dem Tode? Die Idee der Reinkarnation* (Frankfurt, 1977), offers an introductory presentation from the Christian standpoint. H. U. von Balthasar, "Seelenwanderung", in idem, *Homo creatus est* (Einsiedeln, 1986), 103–20 (= *Skizzen zur Theologie*, vol. v), offers a very rich and amply documented theological evaluation.

Chapter VI

LIVING THE TRANSITION:
DEATH AND HOMECOMING
IN THE LIGHT OF
THE ANCIENT RITUAL OF DEATH

In our previous reflections, we have continually encountered a menacing "eschatological amnesia" that forgets
our status as pilgrims, our "citizenship in the heavens"
(Phil 3:20), so that hope in life after death becomes slug-
gish. But we have seen the consequences of this forgetting; if Christ is recalled only as the "historical Jesus" and
not as the Lord of this and of the coming world and time
who is exalted "to the right hand of the Father", then his
image fades to the vague outlines of an exemplary man
of the past (cf. Chapter 1). A Church that is seen in only
temporal and earthly terms and not also at the same time
as heavenly-eternal becomes rigid in the lifeless banality
of a mere organization (cf. Chapter 3). A living hope in
life after death, however, determines a responsibility for
life here on earth that can make renunciations for the
sake of the common good because the brief earthly life is
lived as a responsible pilgrimage (cf. Chapter 4) and is
not clung to as the final goal.

Such an *existence in transition* is possible only where death is not suppressed from view as the *transitus* from this life to the next. Spiritual masters of earlier ages reminded one to think every day of one's own death. Such a recollection is not meant to be a morbid brooding: it is meant to keep awake our knowledge that every day can be our last day and that therefore every day and every hour are precious and unique. But how are we to remember our own death, when death has been very largely suppressed from our view? "Death has become the most trenchant prohibition of the modern world." [1] It is of course true that this suppression of death is at least beginning to change; people are beginning once again to speak of dying and of death, even if only hesitantly. For in the meanwhile we have become largely speechless: we lack the gestures and rites, the symbols and images, that would permit us to deal with dying. It is therefore not surprising that there is renewed interest in earlier generations' customs and rites in connection with death. How did men "go home" in earlier times; how did they live the transition? [2]

[1] Philippe Ariès, *Studien zur Geschichte des Todes im Abendland* (Munich and Vienna, 1976), 173.

[2] One could mention many books besides the works of P. Ariès. Let us select three ethnological studies: J. Zihlmann's impressive documentation *Wie sie heimgingen* (Hitzkirchen, Switzerland: Comenius-Verlag, 1982); Regula Bochsler, "Sterbebräuche und ihr Wandel in der Gemeinde Oberwil (Kanton Aargau)", in *Schweizerisches Archiv für Volkskunde* 79 (1983), 151–74; I. Baumer, "Der Tod—aus der Sicht der Volkskunde", in *Reformatio* 27 (1978), 637–42.

Our reflection here is limited to asking the Church's ancient ritual of death about the vision of "homecoming" that it expresses. What images are employed to speak of this "homecoming", and what gestures surround it? We are not guided here by an interest in the history of the liturgy—we do not seek to give a genetic presentation of the Catholic Church's ritual of death. We wish simply to listen to what was expressed here. Unfortunately, there is only a weak echo of this in the renewed postconciliar ritual.

1. The Liturgy of the Transition (*Transitus*)

From earliest times,[3] the Church celebrates the dying of a Christian as a transition.[4] Following the model of the death of Jesus, which is called an "exodus" in the Gospel of Luke (9:31), Christian dying too is seen as a departure from this world in order to enter through death into the promised land, into paradise. This "rite of transition" has many similarities to the death rites of other religions. The new Christian interpretation of dying does not completely dissolve these common elements. For all men, in all cultures, it is the great transitions of life, such as birth, marriage, and death, that are celebrated in a particular manner. Rituals help one to en-

---

[3] Cf. D. Sicard, *La liturgie de la mort dans l'église latine des origines à la réforme carolingienne* (Münster, 1978) (= LQF vol. 63).

[4] P. Rouillard, "Die Liturgie des Todes als Übergangsritus", in *Concilium* 14 (1978), 111–16.

dure the uncertainties and dangers of these transitions; they give the change and the new situations their meaning and locate them within a larger context that is ordained from on high. As the sociologist of religion P. M. Zulehner says, rites are "vehicles into the world of God".[5] Thus it is not by chance that precisely the transition that leads out of this world into the other, from life on earth to life beyond the grave, has been ritualized with especial intensity. Rather, it is astonishing that our own age stands so helpless when confronted with this decisive turning point in life.

The rite of the Dominican Order[6] had preserved a particularly beautiful and solemn form of the liturgy of death. Here all the phases of dying were very consciously carried out liturgically in an impressive manner. After the Council of Trent, the Roman liturgy simplified the rites but also excised many precious elements, even fewer of which have remained after the most recent liturgical reform. We pose our questions in what follows, then, to the Dominican ritual of the *commendatio animae in transitu fratris* ("recommendation of the soul at the departure of a brother").[7]

---

[5] *Heirat, Geburt, Tod. Eine Pastoral der Lebenswenden* (Vienna, Freiburg, and Basel, 1976), 244.

[6] I quote from the *Processionarium juxta ritum sacri ordinis praedicatorum* of 1930, which reproduces virtually unaltered the archetype of the Dominican liturgy of 1254: cf. H.-R. Philippeau, "La liturgie dominicaine des malades, des mourants et des morts", in *Archives d'Histoire dominicaine* 1 (1946; the only fascicle that appeared), 38–52.

[7] In the Processional of 1930 (cf. n. 6), 170–219.

This rite is in practice no longer celebrated in monasteries; here, too, dying in a hospital has become "normal". One must have a stroke if he is to die at home now! Even in monasteries, death is to a large extent no longer a liturgical event but a clinical affair. The place where one lives and the place where one dies have been separated, and this means that death itself has largely departed from the monasteries. It is not surprising that this is not without consequences for life. But let us turn now to the *commendatio animae*.

If a brother is near death, all the brethren of the monastery are quickly summoned. They gather around the dying man and begin to recite the Litany of the Saints: "Father in heaven, have mercy on him"; "All you saints, pray for him." The saints are asked for their intercession in a long list. If the moment of death has not yet come, sections from the history of the Lord's Passion are read to the dying man. If the dying man can no longer speak, the priest speaks on his behalf the *protestationes*, in which he professes his faith, his willingness to die, his will to be faithful even in the temptations of the death agony: he makes this profession before his guardian angel and before all who stand around him.

When the agony begins, prayers are read in his presence that refer to Christ's suffering and death. Mary is appealed to for consolation and help. When it can be seen that death is imminent, the priest addresses him directly with the tremendous, mighty words of the *Proficis-*

cere, anima christiana:[8] "Depart, Christian soul, from this world, in the name of God the Father the Almighty, who created you; in the name of Jesus Christ, the Son of the living God, who suffered for you; in the name of the Holy Spirit, who was poured out upon you": but the nine choirs of angels and the throngs of saints are mentioned, too: "[depart] in the name of all the saints of God. May your dwelling today be in peace and your home in holy Zion." Thus the dying man is adjured to *depart* now, as if the main thing was not to delay in the moment of the transition, not to be tardy, but to leave this world courageously in the name of God and of all the saints.[9] The fact that a specific exhortation is required here ought to give us food for thought. In the *Proficiscere*, the concepts of which go back to the first Christian centuries,[10] there is expressed the knowledge that death is the departure for the great journey and that God himself summons to this departure through the priest: *de hoc saeculo migrare iussisti* ("You have ordered us to depart from this world"), says another ritual.[11]

---

[8] On the age, form, and transmission of the *Proficiscere*, cf. Sicard, *La liturgie*, 361–68 (with bibliography); it is incomprehensible why the official German translation (in *Die Feier der Krankensakramente* [Einsiedeln et al., 1975], 100f.) painstakingly avoids speaking of the *soul*; the German translation has "kept the soul" in the prayer *Subvenite* (ibid., 103).

[9] Why does the German translation omit *de hoc mundo*? This makes us lose the dramatic element of "being sent off on the journey" from this world, without which it is not possible to go to meet God.

[10] Sicard, *La liturgie*, 368.

[11] The ritual of Pope Adrian, quoted by Sicard, *La liturgie*, 402.

As if wishing to give greater emphasis to the encouragement to set out on the great journey, the priest addresses the dying man once again and gives him recommendations to take with him for the goal of his journey: "I recommend you, beloved brother, to the Almighty God, to him whose creature you are . . . and when your soul now departs from the body, may the glorious flock of angels hasten to meet it!" All the choirs of saints are named, and all of them are to come to meet the one who is coming home: "May blessed peace lull you in the bosom of the patriarchs; . . . may the holy Virgin and Mother of God Mary turn her eyes to you, full of gracious love; may the countenance of Christ Jesus appear mild and festive to you."

But the *commendatio* is also familiar with the dangers of the path on which the soul is now setting out. This is why the priest encourages the dying man: "May you pay no heed to all that is terrible in the darkness, . . . may the abominable Satan with his fellow warriors retreat before you: may he shudder when you arrive, accompanied by the angels, and may he go aside into the dreadful chaos of the eternal night. . . . So may Christ, who died for you, free you from the everlasting death. May Christ, the Son of the living God, give you rest forever on the delightful green pastures [*amoena virentia*] of his paradise. . . . May you see your Redeemer face to face."

The world of these images has almost disappeared.

And yet it awakens in us, as from afar, a deep yearning. We recall Fra Angelico's saints dancing with the angels. Are we no longer capable of appreciating such images? Or do we simply underestimate ourselves?

The liturgy of the great transition continues: in a long prayer like a litany, God is asked to receive his servant in the place of the hoped-for salvation and to rescue him from all the perils of the underworld, as once he rescued the great righteous ones: Enoch and Noah, Abraham, Job, Isaac and Lot, Moses and Daniel, the three young men in the fiery furnace, Susanna, David, Peter and Paul and the holy martyr Thecla: all of these were saved out of great tribulation. From the beginnings of Christian art—which was of course primarily funeral art—we are acquainted with most of these rescues as images of the hope that one will be rescued from the snares of death.

The liturgy reaches a new stage when the brother has died. What a contrast to today's customs at a death! Everything is not finished with the *exitus*. The dead man is not immediately "removed" now that technology has nothing left to do. The earthly path is at an end, but not the fellowship of faith and of love. The homecoming soul is accompanied in intense prayer. The attention of the assembled community is directed to the invisible but real event that begins with the departure of the brother from his earthly life.

Immediately after the decease, all pray the moving *Subvenite*: "Hasten to help, you saints of God! Hasten here, you angels of God! Receive his soul and present it to the face of the Most High!" The great exodus Psalm 113 follows: "When Israel departed from Egypt, and Jacob's house from an alien people . . ." For the exodus "into the land of promise, of light and peace" has just begun. The goal is Christ, and so the assembled brethren pray for the one who has now set out: "May Christ, who has summoned you, receive you: may the angels lead you to Abraham's bosom."

The Liturgy of the *transitus* is not yet over. The corpse, clothed in the religious habit, is laid out in the church (and not in the refrigerated mortuaries in the hospital cellar, as is usual today!). It is explicitly stated that the superior is to see to it that the corpse does not remain alone: until the burial, confrères keep watch in prayer by the dead man. But not even the burial breaks the bond of unity. The deceased brother is regularly remembered. The community grows out beyond the threshold of death and gathers at the goal of the pilgrimage.

The spirit of this liturgy of transition is most impressively expressed in the Gregorian chant of the *Requiem*. A contemporary composer has said: "Is not this a cradle song?" The dramatic accents are not lacking in the liturgy of death. Through all the mourning and pain, the fundamental tone is peaceful and full of consolation. Only one who sees dying in the light of Easter morning can sing in this way.

2. *Ars Moriendi* as an Aid to Living

What is the use of this much abbreviated account of a
ritual of death that is scarcely practiced any longer? The
point is something very simple: in the helplessness with
which we confront death today, it is important to take a
fresh look at ancient signs and forgotten words in order
to learn step by step anew from them how dying can
rediscover its place in life. Let us attempt to "hear"
something.

a. *Dying as a Human Celebration*

Dying loses its speechlessness when it is not reduced to
a biological misfortune but is celebrated as a *human*
event. There is no more eloquent proof of the failure of
materialism than its panicked helplessness in the face of
death. If death is merely the irreparable final stasis of the
machine that is the body, then it is only logical that
dying is swept aside into the anonymity of a clinic. It is
only when considered from this materialistic view that a
sudden, painless, and unnoticed death can be called "a
beautiful death". For centuries, Christians have prayed
that God might preserve them from sudden and unpre-
pared death: *ab impraevisa morte libera nos, Domine!* It was
counted as a real misfortune to be taken by surprise by
death suddenly and without receiving the sacraments of
the dying.

The primary motivation of the prayer for "a good

death" and of the wish not to die without "the consola-
tions of the Church" was scarcely "fear of hell".
Rather, this shows a knowledge of the importance of
this moment and of the necessity of preparing oneself
for it. The hour of death can, however, be taken so seriously only when it is awaited as the *transition* into eternal life. This may sound banal, but it is heavy with
consequences: death will become human once again
only to the extent that it is seen and lived as the gate-
way to eternal life. Our contemporary (bad) customs
connected with death are the most eloquent indication
that we have lost a strong relatedness to life beyond
death. The stasis of a machine is not celebrated: it is
merely registered.

b. *Dangers of the Transition*

Behind the concern to live the transition well prepared
and as something embedded in ritual lies a knowledge
of the importance of this transition and therefore of the
dangers involved. What is said about this in the Christian rite has numerous parallels in the myths and rites of
many peoples.[12] Why else was the attempt made in ancient Egypt with all care to make easier the path of the
dead "across to the other world" and to ensure its
safety, if not because they knew that the transition is

---

[12] An initial overview: G. Stephenson (ed.), *Leben und Tod in den Re-
ligionen. Symbol und Wirklichkeit* (Darmstadt, 1980).

full of danger? The rite of transition is to help the dead person not to miss the path into life. In his dialogue *Phaedo*, Plato transmits a detailed myth of life beyond death, beginning with the assertion that it is not as Aeschylus describes it, so that "only one simple footpath leads into the underworld". "But I believe", says Socrates, "that the path is neither one nor single. Otherwise, one would not need any guide, for it is not possible to go astray anywhere, if there is only one path." But *de facto*, the path into the underworld bifurcates repeatedly, and this is why the dead man also has a companion, a *daimôn* who leads him along this dangerous path.[13] For the Greeks, Hermes is the *psychopompos*, the "leader of souls", into the life beyond the grave.

In the Christian liturgy, it is especially the angels, but also the saints, who lead the soul into paradise. According to the Christian liturgy, it is the demons, the devil and his cohorts, who are the source of the terrors of this "journey of the soul" that many myths describe: the demons want to terrify, oppress, and corrupt the soul as it comes home. Without the "protective accompaniment" of the "heavenly hosts", the soul would be lost.

The world of images of the myths—from the Egyptian book of the dead to the Tibetan, from the Greek myths to the Christian rite—is in astonishing agreement on this point. Is our age's lack of understanding in the

---

[13] *Phaedo* 107d–8a; cf. J. Pieper, *Über die platonischen Mythen* (Munich, 1965), 36–46.

face of these testimonies to have more weight than their impressive common accord? To dismiss all this with a reference to a "superseded image of the world" means not necessarily that our age is more enlightened about these "last things" of man but rather that an ancient wisdom about life that was common to mankind at an earlier time has been lost to us today.[14]

c. *Transition as Judgment*

The ancient rites were familiar with the dangers of the transition. The threat to the soul in its homecoming is derived not only from the outside, from the hostile powers, but above all from within, for the innermost dimension is laid bare in death. No external appearance, no mere human goodwill helps anymore. The soul stands there naked and bare. *Quid sum miser tunc dicturus?* ("What shall I, wretched man, say, then—before the judge?"), as the mighty chant of the *Dies Irae* (a victim of a surely too rationalistic reform of the liturgy) put it. Here too, the myths bear witness to a universal human experience, which is not cleared away in Christianity but is "preserved".

---

[14] Why does the present formulation of the prayers for the dying (cf. n. 8 above and also no. 79 in the Church hymnal *Gotteslob*) not mention this dangerous and dark side of the "transition" with one single word? Such a silence can lead to people seeking help in coping with these experiences no longer in the sphere of the Church but in the sphere of the occult or superstition.

The dead person stands in all the nakedness of his misery on the threshold to the life beyond death. What can he present in his favor; how can he authenticate himself? The transition is judgment, for in the stripping of death it is the entire life that is laid bare. Plato has caught this in a powerful mythical image in the *Gorgias*. "On the meadow at the crossroads, where the two paths diverge, the one to the island of the blessed, the other to Tartarus", are the souls of the dead judged. So Socrates relates, and continues: "Death, it seems to me, is nothing other than the separation of two things, the soul and the body." [15] But just as the corpse retains traces of life, for example, the scars of earlier wounds, the same is true of the soul.

> Everything in the soul is visible, when it is stripped of the body . . . when it now comes before the judge . . . , he places it before himself and looks at the soul of each one, without knowing whose it is. But often, when he has the great king before him, or other kings or princes, he finds nothing healthy in the soul: he finds it thoroughly scourged and full of blisters of perjury and unrighteousness, just as each one has left on the soul the mark of his way of life; he finds everything dislocated by lies and arrogance, and nothing straight, because it grew up without truth. Rather, the soul reveals itself to be full of disproportion and ugliness because of all the violence and insipidity,

[15] *Gorgias*, 524ab; J. Pieper shows that the definition has not lost anything of its substantial validity: *Tod und Unsterblichkeit* (Munich, 1968), chap. III.

presumption and excess in what it has done. As soon as he
sees such a soul, he sends it without honor straight into
the prison, where it will endure what is coming to it. . . .
But if he meanwhile sees another soul that has lived a holy
life in the truth, the soul of a man who lived alone by
himself or of someone else—but above all, I think, O Callicles, the soul of one who loves wisdom, who has at-
tended to his own affairs and not done much else beyond
that—then he rejoices and sends it to the island of the
blessed.[16]

d. *Life in Transition*

The knowledge that speaks out of the myth—and Socrates says that he himself takes it to be not a fable (*mu-
thos*) but the truth (*logos*)[17]—is the knowledge that the
homecoming is judgment and that the moment of
death means the hour of truth. Socrates deduces from
this that he wants to *live* already now in such a way that
he can "appear before the judge with a soul as healthy
as possible".[18] The dangers of the transition are the
same as the dangers of life. Life is revealed in dying, and
this is why the *ars bene moriendi* consists in the *ars bene
vivendi*. And Socrates says this to the sophist Callicles,
the man of success, to whom profit is more important
than value and power more than the good: "Listen to

---

[16] *Gorgias*, 525a–26c.
[17] Ibid., 523a.
[18] Ibid., 526d.

me and follow me to the place where you will be more happy in life and in death." [19]

The Christian tradition does not speak any differently. The Church prays in the Preface of the Mass for the dead: "For those who believe in you, Lord, life is not taken away, but transformed." Death as transformation: this is possible only if this transformation has already begun *before* bodily death. The great Byzantine "lay theologian" *Nicolas Cabasilas* (fourteenth century) understood how to say this with an impressive clarity that is seldom encountered. In the first chapter of his book *On Life in Christ*, he shows that we already form in *this* life the "organs" for eternal life, by beginning to live "in Christ":

> Life in Christ comes into being in the present life and begins thence. But it is perfected in the coming life, after we have entered that Day. And if it has not already begun here, neither the present existence nor even future existence is able to bestow that life in Christ on the souls of men in its perfected state. For fleshly existence spreads darkness in the present life, and this gloom and transiency cannot inherit imperishability. This is why Paul thought it better to depart and be with Christ, for he says: "It is far better to depart and be with Christ" (Phil 1:23).
>
> But nothing more can bring to bliss those whom the coming aeon finds without the powers and senses that are necessary for that life; they will dwell, dead and unhappy, in that blissful and immortal world. The Logos, the light,

[19] Ibid., 527c.

does indeed arise for them, and the sun gives its pure ray: but it is no longer possible for an eye to be formed. The precious fragrance of the Pneuma flows forth and fills all things: but the one who has no sense of smell then will never receive a new sense of smell. On that Day, his friends are permitted to share with the Son of God in his mysteries: and they are permitted to hear from him what he himself has heard from the Father. But it is only those who are already his friends and have ears that attain to that place. For it is not first there that friendship is made, that the ear is opened, the nuptial garment made ready and all the rest prepared that is fitting for that Bridegroom: *no, the present life is the workshop for all of this.* And one who does not already possess these things before his decease will have no share in that life. The five virgins (Mt 25:1–12) and the one who was invited to the wedding (Mt 22:1–14) bear witness to this. After they arrived without oil, or without a nuptial garment, it was no longer possible for them to get this for themselves.

This world bears in its womb the man who is inwardly wholly new and created in accordance with God. And if he is formed and shaped here, then, when he has become perfect, he will be born into that perfected and eternally young cosmos.[20]

To live the transition thus means to have already passed over from death to life. It is love alone that effects such a transition: "We know that we have passed over from death into life, because we love the brethren. Anyone

[20] PG 150, 493 B – 496; German trans. (cf. note 82 of previous chapter), 15f.

who does not love remains in death" (1 Jn 3:14). Nicolas Cabasilas closes his book *On Life in Christ* with this indestructible power of love in view:

> What therefore could have a more proper right to the name "life" than love? And besides this, that which alone is left when everything is taken away, that which does not allow the living to die, is life. But this is how love is. For, as Paul says, when everything else is destroyed in the new aeon, then love alone remains (1 Cor 13:8), and it is sufficient for that life in Christ Jesus our Lord, to whom all glory belongs, Amen.[21]

---

[21] Ibid., bk. VII: PG 150, 725 D; German trans., 246.

ACKNOWLEDGMENT

Before being published in the German edition, *Existenz im Übergang: Pilgerschaft, Reinkarnation, Vergöttlichung*, some of the chapters in this book were previously published in other forms. A list, by chapter, follows:

1. " 'Gott will für ewig Mensch bleiben.' Anmerkungen zur Auslegungsgeschichte des Glaubensartikels 'Sedet ad dexteram Patris' ", in *IKZ Communio* 13 (1984), 1–13.

2. "L'homme est-il fait pour devenir Dieu? Notes sur le sens chrétien de la 'déification' ou 'divinisation' de l'homme", in *Omnis Terra* 22 (1983), 53–64 (German trans. by H. U. von Balthasar).

3. "L'Eglise de la terre, le Royaume de Dieu et l'Eglise du ciel", in *Esprit et Vie* 96, no. 50 (1986), 689–97 (German trans. by Dr. A. Berz).

4. Hitherto published only privately.

5. First section: "Quelques notes sur l'attitude de la théologie paléochrétienne face à la réincarnation", in C.-A. Keller (ed.), *La réincarnation. Théories, raisonnements et appréciations* (Berne, 1986), 159–80 (German trans. by Dr. A. Berz).

   Second section: a revised version of "La réincarnation: un défi pour le christianisme", in *Choisir* no. 297, September 1984, 6–9.

6. Previously unpublished.

INDEX